Jazz Mergirl

The True Story of Jazz Jennings,
a Transgender Girl Born in a Boy's Body

Bruce Edlen, M.A.ed

Jazz Mergirl is in tribute to Jazz and the Jennings family.
Although not an authorized biography,
profits from this book will be donated to the
TransKids Purple Rainbow Foundation.

First Edition

ISBN (soft cover): 978-1-5153-2826-1
ISBN (e-book) Pending

Dedicated to
Jazz, Jeanette, and Greg Jennings.
You inspired me to write this book.

Be who you are,
And say what you feel,
Because those who mind don't matter,
And those who matter don't mind.
– Dr. Seuss –

I am a soccer player. I am an artist. I am a high schooler. I
am transgender. I am proud. I am Jazz!
~ Jazz Jennings ~

~Jazz Mergirl~

~Jazz Mergirl~

Contents

~Jazz Mergirl~

v

~Jazz Mergirl~

Preface

I had no idea I was going to write a book – *this* book. And then, when I did begin this project, I had no idea that it would take more than a year of research and writing to bring *Jazz Mergirl* to publication. Jazz jokingly told me I probably know more about her life than she does!

It all started after I ended my 20-year career as a teacher, and was casting about for my next big venture. I knew it was going to be something creative, but what? Then one day, while browsing around on YouTube, I happened across "My Secret Self," a Barbara Walters television program I vaguely remembered having first seen in 2007.

I spent the next 45 minutes engrossed in a most compelling and touching story about children who are known as *transgender*, including six-year-old Jazz Jennings. This was a topic related to gender that I didn't know much about or even think about until I once again saw the videocast on YouTube.

On the other hand, my master's thesis from years before was on the subject of gender equity, an issue I thought about daily in my own interactions with students. I had also conducted teacher workshops based on my thesis. So I was naturally interested and fascinated by this television documentary.

After viewing that program, I watched a few related YouTube selections, and searched Google for more information about Jazz Jennings. When I looked online hoping to purchase a biography about Jazz, there was an announcement of a children's picture book titled *I Am Jazz*, to be published in September 2014. But besides that one children's title, there were no other Jazz Jennings biographies. Although I didn't find the lengthier book I was looking for, I did buy *I Am Jazz* upon its release, (which Jazz autographed for me).

My explorations had located a wealth of online material about Jazz Jennings, and what it means to be transgender. However, I noticed that the only relevant books I found were fiction titles for very young children, a few guidebooks for their parents, and a number of biographies about transgender adults. My web search turned up no non-fiction publications concerning transgender kids written for young teens, and there was little available at the older teen level (although that's now beginning to change).

Yet it is this age group, the younger *Millennials* and *Generation Z*, that is leading the way for society to become more open-minded and accepting of the LGBTQ community. A growing number of trans kids now feel more confident in "coming out" to their families, friends, and beyond.

The teacher in me recognized this situation as providing both a need and an opportunity. I soon realized I wanted to write the book that I hadn't been able to find. I was motivated to share this fascinating and moving true story about Jazz and the Jennings family. At the same time, I wanted to inform and enlighten readers about people who are transgender and to further the cause of the Jennings' TransKids Purple Rainbow Foundation. *Jazz Mergirl's* profits will be donated to support the foundation.

Although I wrote *Jazz Mergirl* for a teen and young adult audience, it will also appeal to interested parents and other grownups. What's more, as the manuscript progressed, it became apparent this book will be of value to additional groups of readers, such as classroom teachers, those in psychology and gender studies programs, therapists, medical students, and others in the healthcare and child protective systems.

As I bring this work to completion, and share it with my readers, I hope you too will be moved and inspired by Jazz's life of courage, determination, and love.

Bruce Edlen
August 2015

~Jazz Mergirl~

Notes to the Reader

Jazz Mergirl incorporates several unique features about which readers should be aware:

1. This book is intended for a wide-range of people, from younger and older teens to adults. To make this book more accessible to those younger teen readers (and anyone else not already familiar with the medical terminology involved), "scaffolds" have been provided along with the specialized vocabulary and concepts discussed. These "helpful hints" will be found enclosed in (parentheses). In addition, an extensive, user-friendly glossary at the end of the book will also serve the same purpose.

2. The subject of human sexuality is quite complex and can be somewhat confusing. After finishing *Jazz Mergirl*, adult readers may find it useful to go over the Guide in Appendix 8, which is a basic and straightforward introduction to that topic.

3. This story includes a significant amount of quotations. These and other references have all been properly attributed. However, to keep these citations from interrupting or distracting the reader, each source is noted in the text with a superscripted number that corresponds to entries in the Bibliography.

4. A number of quotations have been slightly modified for the purpose of clarity. To that end, inconsistent and confusing use of the pronouns *he* and *she* were corrected in quotations taken from family interviews.

5. On occasion, a word or phrase was changed or added to a quotation, again for clarity, but no [brackets] were emplaced around these adjustments. That was to reduce distractions for younger and older readers alike. For the same reason, when words were deleted from original quotations, the traditional ellipses (…) were not employed.

6. Great care was taken when making these minor modifications so that the speakers' original meaning and intent were preserved.

7. In the first part of the story, Jazz is referred to with male terms (*boy, he, him*), while later in the book, these transition to female words (*girl, she, her*). This was done to show the actual sequence of events, and to be as clear and consistent as possible.

8. Readers may notice throughout this book the use of the "singular pronoun" *they*, in place of *he* or *she*. This singular pronoun is now often used in English to be more gender-inclusive, especially when the person being referred to is of indeterminate gender.

9. A decision was made to spell the plural of the family name as *Jennings*, rather than the more correct, but awkward *Jenningses*. The same applies to the possessive form, *Jennings'*.

10. Being *transgender* is a relatively new topic in both the healthcare and science fields, and for discussion within society as a whole. In recent years, it has been the subject of much debate, including within the LGBTQ community itself. As a result, the terminology used is evolving, and it too is subject to much discussion and debate. Keeping that in mind, the vocabulary and language employed in *Jazz Mergirl* is as accurate and up-to-date as possible. When writing this book, the GLAAD *Guide* for journalists was a most useful resource.

11. In this same regard, every effort has been made to portray events and present quotations, terminology, and explanations in as correct and accurate a manner as possible. Any errors reported to the author will be addressed in subsequent printings and editions, as necessary.

12. One final note: While this is a work of nonfiction, the names of some individuals and their locations have been altered or masked in order to respect and protect the privacy and well-being of all concerned. This includes using the pseudonym *Jennings*.

~Jazz Mergirl~

Introduction

On Friday, April 27, 2007, about seven million viewers tuned in to a one-hour Barbara Walters *20/20* TV program titled "My Secret Self." Six-year-old Jazz Jennings and her family were featured, alongside two other families raising children known as *transgender*. Barbara explained that, although born with a boy body, in her mind Jazz identified as being a girl. Simply put, being transgender means that a person does not identify with the gender they were assigned at birth. Relatively few people had heard about this condition in adults, much less a child this young. In fact, Jazz was diagnosed around the age of three, one of the youngest-identified transgender children as of that time.[94]

Many of the TV viewers were taken with this sweet, shy, and adorable little child. Her deepest, heartfelt yearning to be recognized and accepted as a girl was now becoming a reality. However, there was an air of sadness about Jazz as she was being interviewed. Perhaps this was a sadness left over from earlier times of struggle, frustration, and hurt that predated her recent transition to girlhood.

A drawing and its caption that Jazz had made the year before, at age five, expressed all of that. As she explained it to Barbara, the little girl in the picture was crying because she wasn't allowed to wear a dress to school. But then, Jazz went on to say, her mom finally *did* let the girl go

1

to school in a dress. Barbara asked, "Is the little girl in the picture you?" to which Jazz simply nodded her head, "Yes." [94]

There was also sadness, but what's more, an inner peace and determination in Jazz, as she sat in her little pink chair and sang to Barbara from Rodgers & Hammerstein's *Cinderella*:

I know of a spot in my house,
Where no one can stand in my way.

In my own little corner,
In my own little chair,
I can be whatever I want to be.

On the wings of my fancy,
I can fly anywhere,
And the world will open its arms to me.

… Just as long as I stay,
In my own little corner,
All alone, in my own little chair.

Fast-forward about six years to January 2013. In a follow-up *20/20* Barbara Walters program titled "Transgender at 11: Listening to Jazz," viewers saw an outgoing, 11-year-old bundle of energy and joy. Was this really the same girl? Asked by Barbara to describe Jazz, her proud mom, Jeanette Jennings, used these adjectives: "Vibrant, happy, full of life, self-confident, beautiful, glowing, so feminine." [95]

This, then, is the story of *Jazz Mergirl*, as she and her family journey on the road to fulfilling her dream of bringing out the girl she knows is inside, and being her authentic self. At the same time, Jazz has made it her goal to teach the world to be more understanding and accepting of those who are, in her words, "born unique and special."

She also wants to help those unique and special kids learn to accept and appreciate themselves, as she has done. When responding to an interviewer's question, Jazz said, "I thought that I was made wrong. But now, I know there's nothing wrong with me. I love myself." [87] In 2014, Jazz wrote in her children's picture book, "I don't mind being different. Different is special! I think what matters most is what a person is like inside. And inside, I am happy. I am Jazz." [30]

Come along and explore Jazz's journey, including the challenges and struggles, and on to fulfillment and happiness. As her father, Greg Jennings, observed, "All parents really want for their children is for them to be happy." [87] And now she is.

~Jazz Mergirl~

Chapter 1
Barbie, Barbie, Barbie!

By the start of the new millennium, Jeanette and Greg Jennings were the proud parents of three wonderful children. The oldest, a quiet and serious girl named Ari (Arial), was age five, and her energetic twin brothers, Griffen and Sander, were three-years-old. The Jennings couple met in their hometown when they were little kids and lived just three houses apart. They became best friends.[87] Today, after over 20 years of marriage, they are still best friends, and a very loving couple.

Although she was sure the family was now complete, Jeanette was in for a big surprise. In early 2000, experiencing some unusual flu-like symptoms, she asked her doctor for a checkup. To her amazement, she found out that another Jennings child was on the way.[84 / 87]

As her pregnancy progressed, Jeanette naturally compared this one to her previous pregnancies. Because it felt identical to the time she was expecting the birth of Ari, Jeanette was certain this baby would be a girl too. So, at about five months, it came as another surprise ("shock, actually") to be told by the doctor that her intuition was incorrect. It was a boy.[84] Although Jeanette didn't care what her baby's gender was, this "mistaken intuition" would prove to be prophetic.

Barbie, Barbie, Barbie!

With the excited and joyful family present, Baby Jennings was born on October 6, 2000. The baby's birth name remained private until a July 2015 TV interview, when Greg Jennings shared that his child's original first name was Jaron.[40.1] The little boy was a very healthy and happy child. Over the next year-and-a-half, he made normal childhood progress, from crawling to walking, and from babbling to talking.

But what was unexpected was his attraction to Ari's girl clothes and toys, and his preference to play with *her*, not the twin boys. Boy-type gifts were consistently rejected, the twins' playthings ignored.[87] This child had a mind of his own. Years later, when reminiscing about those times, Jazz said, "As soon as I could crawl, I would reach for girl toys."[36.1] "I was forever raiding my sister's dress-up chest and her closet. And you could always find me dolled-up like a mermaid or princess, wearing wigs, beaded necklaces, and those plastic high heels from the Disney Store." [44]

Family videos show the 15-month-old diapered toddler clunking around the house in Ari's sparkly plastic heels. According to Jeanette, her child "loved Barbie dolls. He surrounded himself with anything pink, sparkly, and beautiful."[35] Pink audiocassette in hand, the youngster asked to hear the music by calling out, "Barbie, Barbie, Barbie!" [94]

Some years later, in a television interview, Dr. Drew Pinsky asked Jeanette, "And Mom, did you go with that from the beginning, or were you resistant, or trying to redirect?" She replied, "I went with it. He was such a lovely baby, so happy. And if he said he wanted to play with something girly, I didn't have a problem with that." [73] "Who cares, you know? We're really open-minded." [28] Jeanette and Greg thought this interest in all things feminine to be just a "developmental phase that would pass." [94]

But it was more than that. Reflecting back on those early times, Jeanette observed that, "From the day he could first express himself, there was nothing male about this child." [94] In a speech given years later, Jazz shared more about that situation. "When I was younger, I was nothing like my older twin brothers or my dad. I wanted to be exactly like my mom and my older sister." [44] Jazz told an interviewer, "I was not happy with the clothes I had to wear and with short hair." [28] At just 15-months of age, this child would even unsnap his "onesies" outfit to make it look more like a dress. [94]

Jazz also recalled that before being able to speak, "I remember no one knew I had a girl brain. [28] "I felt like a girl, and I felt uncomfortable in my body." [78] "I remember being upset with how people treated me." [41] Summing up these memories, Jazz said, "I didn't just like girly things. I *knew* I was a *girl* trapped in a boy's body." [36.1]

Jeanette explained to one television journalist that her child "was really verbal when around two." As soon as he was able to make himself understood, the toddler stated emphatically, "Mommy, I'm a girl, *not* a boy. There's a mistake. I'm in the wrong body." [68] To skeptics, Jeanette responds, "Yet, I know a lot of people think, a two-year-old doesn't say these things. But he did!" [68]

7

"He would get angry when we referred to him as a boy," Jeanette told another interviewer.[1] Whenever Mom said, "Good boy," the youngster's retort was always, "No, Mommy. Good *girl!*" Explaining how she dealt with this situation, Jeanette said, "I just didn't want him to feel bad, so I said, okay, you're a girl. Fine." [73]

One day, when about two-and-a-half-years old, the toddler awoke from a dream. He came up to Mom and told her that in the dream, the Good Fairy had waved a magic wand and changed his penis into a vagina. "When will I get my vagina?" he asked.[87] Jeanette was shocked. She later said of her reaction to this question that she felt "just numb, frozen." [94] "You're like, this is not typical. This is not something a normal child would do." [28]

Over time, that same sort of question would be repeated, such as asking Mom and Dad when would his private parts match his sister's? [84] As the months went by, Jeanette realized that her son's insistence his "penis was a mistake," and that he was a girl, was *not* turning out to be a "developmental phase" that would go away. In fact, this pattern of behavior became more insistent and persistent, and was a genuine, ongoing mental-health concern. Jeanette explained it this way: "A phase is called a phase because it is just that. It ends. And this was not ending. This was getting stronger." [94]

Meanwhile, Dad was not processing his son's unusual behavior in the same way as Jeanette. In these situations, fathers are often the last to grasp and accept the difficult concept that their child is not developing in the same manner that most children do. Dads want their boys to be boys (or girls to be girls). A few years later, as he thought back, Greg Jennings acknowledged that he had not understood the import of what was going on with his son's behavior. "At first, I was oblivious. And then, once I started to see him gravitate towards typically what a girl would gravitate to, I was in denial. I really didn't want to accept it." [68]

But Jeanette was *not* in denial. She was more perplexed and concerned, and unsure what to do.

~Jazz Mergirl~

Chapter 2

Gender Identity Disorder

As it happened, Jeanette Jennings had earned a master's degree in clinical counseling, so it was natural for her to begin researching the cause of her child's remarkable ways. Back in those days, the Internet didn't provide much help to Jeanette. However, it turned out the answer was right there on her bookshelf, in a text called *The DSM.*[*] This is a thick reference book used by psychologists and other healthcare professionals to help determine specific mental health issues.

Flipping through the pages, Jeanette soon came upon a section of the book about something she'd never heard of called *Gender Identity Disorder*, now known as *Gender Dysphoria* (discontent). She was stunned because her little boy met *all* of the key indicators for this condition.[94]

Put in nonmedical terms, Jeanette's child: (1) insisted he was of the opposite gender, a girl, (2) he was determined to act like a girl, (3) he insisted on wearing girl clothes (4) he most wanted to have friends and playmates who were girls, (5) and he expressed a strong desire to play games and have toys most associated with girls. In summary, this child

---

[*] *Diagnostic and Statistical Manual of Mental Disorders.*

had a strong and consistent identification with the opposite gender,[90] a situation commonly referred to as being *transgender*.

According to the *DSM*, there are two additional indicators that are required to confirm gender dysphoria. The person's birth-assigned sex causes "a persistent discomfort" (dysphoria), and this discomfort leads to "significant distress or impairment" for the individual.[94] This certainly was the case with the Jennings' child. To be clear, some individuals who are transgender do *not* experience gender dysphoria. But that wasn't the situation with this youngster.

Dr. Johanna Olson, a doctor of adolescent medicine at Children's Hospital in Los Angeles, specializes in youth with gender dysphoria. Dr. Olson states that she always refers to a set of three words to guide her judgment: *insistent, consistent,* and *persistent.* The Jennings' son fervently *insisted* he was a girl, not a boy. He was *consistent* in expressing the same notion over and over again, saying that his body was a mistake, and that he wanted this fault to be fixed. And the little boy certainly was *persistent.* He just never gave up. In fact, children who are diagnosed with gender dysphoria and continue to experience these intense feelings through adolescence, are sometimes referred to as *persisters.*[8]

*****

Dr. Marvin Belzer is an internationally recognized leader in the field of transgender care for youth, and Director of the Division of Adolescent and Young Adult Medicine at Children's Hospital Los Angeles. He and Dr. Olson work together. Dr. Belzer points out that, of course, children are not exactly alike, and so all three of these gender-dysphoria markers may or may not be present at the same time. Nor will these indicators be experienced in the same manner, from one child to the next.[4.1] Not all children are as strong-willed as Jazz, and may very well conform, and repress their true sense of self, especially if they tend to be "people-pleasers."

It is a parent's responsibility to be observant of their child's words and behaviors, remain open-minded, and be accepting and supportive of what that child says and expresses as being their authentic self. This is what unconditional love is all about, as Jeanette and Greg Jennings demonstrate every day with their own family.

At the same time that parents are being accepting and supportive of their children, Dr. Belzer cautions them not to "jump to conclusions."[4.1] Most young kids go through a time of exploring their gender identities. They experiment with stereotypical gender-conventional behavior, as well as cross-gender play, such as boys putting on dresses and nail polish, and girls pretending to be super heroes. And for most of those children, it is just that, experimenting. Some even go through brief periods or "phases" of expression, like wanting to dress and go by a name typical of a gender different than assigned at birth. This could go on for a few days or even a few weeks.

On the other hand, there are those rare young children like Jazz Jennings who go well-beyond just experimenting and "going through phases." This unusual situation persists for weeks and months (six months is a commonly used "rule of thumb"), and is often accompanied by insistent behaviors and expressions around gender-identity issues. This may or may not include some degree of social dysfunction and serious, even debilitating, gender dysphoria.[4.1]

At this point, some parents make an assumption that their child is transgender, and may then make life-changing decisions based on that supposition. However, not all children are ready for or want to move beyond this initial stage of development.[4.1] Besides, the parents might be mistaken about their youngster's situation. This could instead be some other form of gender variance, from the child being *gender-expressive*, to *gender-fluid*, to simply being a more effeminate boy or "tom-boyish" girl. (For more information, see Appendix 8 and the Glossary.)

And finally, some doctors and therapists say there is the possibility that for a small number of these unique children, their unusual behaviors and expressions may *desist* (stop) over time. At present, it's impossible to predict with any degree of certainty if and when this might occur. That is because there is little in the way of reliable research data available to answer this and numerous other questions about these youths.[4.1]

At long last, some well-designed, ongoing, long-term investigative studies are now being conducted, but it will be years before they yield useful information. In the meantime, reports from knowledgeable gender therapists who work with young transgender children indicate very few of these kids actually desist ("change their minds"). [87.1]

Since there are so many complex variables associated with identifying and treating transgender and gender-variant children, Dr. Belzer recommends parents search for knowledgeable professionals who can help guide them along this very uncertain path. Rather than jump to those conclusions, it is time to locate expert help and guidance.[4.1]

Parents or other caregivers are advised to be especially careful when selecting a gender therapist or other counselor. They should choose someone who is skilled in working with transgender and other gender-variant youth. Be aware that some therapists still adhere to the now-discredited "conversion therapy" or "reparative therapy" model. This approach claims to "fix" such a child, but instead has been reported to be quite harmful. Marlo Mack, parent of a transgender daughter, speaks from experience when she urges others to seek guidance from a counselor who is supportive and practices an "affirming model" of therapy.[60.1]

One thing is for sure. Doing nothing can be as damaging as proceeding without professional assistance. Both Dr. Belzer and Dr. Olson state they know from years of clinical practice that "doing nothing with children and youth with severe dysphoria is not the same as doing no harm. Doing nothing can be extremely harmful." [4.1]

*****

After reading about the startling diagnosis in the *DSM* textbook, Jeanette and Greg Jennings' next step was to take their child, now three-years-old, to visit the family's pediatrician. The doctor thought Jeanette was correct about this being a case of gender identity disorder, and recommended they see a professional who specializes in such matters. As Jeanette later shared, she was so taken aback, "My mouth opened up, and you literally had to scrape me off the floor." [94] It was one thing to read and conjecture about information found in a healthcare manual, but quite another to hear that same diagnosis confirmed by a medical practitioner.

Jeanette observed that, "No parent wants to hear their child has any disorder." Her stomach did flip-flops as she fretted over her son's problematic future. Would he be accepted and loved, or bullied and shunned? [84] This medical finding was "something difficult to come to terms with, because it could be a very hard life" for her child. [71]

Shortly thereafter, the Jennings took their little one to an appointment with a highly-recommended gender therapist, Dr. Marilyn Volker. The doctor conducted an extensive, one-hour interview. While they were talking, if Dr. Volker used the "wrong" pronoun *he*, the youngster immediately objected, saying, "I'm a girl. I'm *she*." [94]

One very informative test that Dr. Volker gave was showing two "anatomically correct" dolls, a boy doll and a girl doll, and asked, "Which doll are you like? Which is like your body?" After pausing to think, the bright child pointed to the male doll and said, "This is me now," and then pointed to the female doll and said, "This is what I want." "Why?" asked the doctor. "Because I'm a girl." [28]

After completing a very thorough exam, Dr. Volker came to the same conclusion as Jeanette and the pediatrician. She said this child was indeed experiencing gender identity disorder (gender dysphoria). At the time, Jazz was probably the youngest child ever to have been diagnosed with this condition.[28] *

For children and adults, being transgender means a person whose *gender identity* in their mind is different from their *physical sex* when born. The person insists they were born into the wrong body.[90 / 94]

Chaz Bono (born to show-business couple Sonny and Cher Bono), who is also transgender, explained it this way to a *New York Times* reporter:

---

*Jazz does not like being referred to with the terms *diagnosed* and *condition*, or *disorder*, because these words suggest there is something wrong with her. She prefers the adjectives *unique* and *special*.

To one journalist she declared, "The dictionary definition of *diagnose* is, 'Identify the nature of an illness or other problem by examination of the symptoms.' Do I look like I have an illness? Do I look like I have a problem? Being transgender is not a problem. It is not an illness. It's just who you are." [81]

There's a gender in your brain and a gender in your body. For 99 percent of people, those things are in alignment. For transgender people, they're mismatched. That's all it is. It's not complicated, it's not a neurosis. It's a mix-up.[98]

Sometimes Jazz says, "I was born a girl trapped in a boy's body." Many other transgender individuals, including adults, also use that word "trapped." As a little child, Jazz knew she was a girl inside herself, but did not know a way to be recognized and accepted by other people as being a girl, not a boy. When she got older, and could clearly express her feelings, Jazz would explain that being transgender means, "I have a girl brain, a boy body, I think like a girl, but I have the different (private) parts." [87] Now she has an even simpler way of explaining her situation: "I was born with a girl brain in a boy body."

This is a good time to briefly address the misunderstanding that many people have in which they confuse *gender identity* with *sexual identity (sexual orientation)*. *Gender identity* develops early on in a child's life, as happened with Jazz. It is the youngster's internal, deeply-held sense in their mind of being a boy or a girl. *Sexual identity* or *sexual orientation*, meaning "to whom a person is attracted," comes about later in life, and has nothing to do with gender identity. (Refer to Appendix 8 at the back of this book for more information about these two facets of human sexuality.)

Chapter 3
Why?

Why did this child, and only a small percentage of the population, turn out to be transgender? (Estimates range from ¼ percent to 1 percent of the general population as being transgender. That's just as few as 2 people up to as many as 10 people out of a thousand.)[*] Within the scientific and medical community, there is a great deal of uncertainty, speculation, and controversy over this "why" question.

Healthcare professionals are not the only ones with questions. Much of the public lack any knowledge at all about people who are transgender or, just as problematic, hold completely false notions about trans individuals. Many even mistakenly believe that parents somehow cause their children to be transgender. In fact, misinformed critics have claimed the Jennings *forced* their child into an unnatural female role because they wanted another daughter. Besides being absurd on the face of it, what caring parents would ever want to bring such a lifetime ordeal onto their child and the whole family, just to have one more daughter?

---

[*]In total, there are an estimated 700,000 transgender adults in the US. The number of trans youth below the age of 18 is more difficult to calculate because so many are unidentified and / or remain in the shadows of society. There may be as many youth as adult transgender individuals, so perhaps the total number within the US is 1.5 million. That's a tiny percent of the total population, but it's still a lot of transgender people.

Why?

Dr. Olson, the adolescent-medicine specialist, states that, "You don't make a decision about your gender identity. It's not something you decide." It's simply how some people come into the world. As Jeanette Jennings vehemently put it, "I didn't do this to my child. This is the way my child was born!" She went on to say, "We didn't force anything on Jazz. This is just how she is, from the very earliest that she could express herself." [94]

Numerous candid videos and photographs taken of Jazz starting at just 15-months-old make it obvious that her gender self-expression comes naturally from within. This conclusion is supported by the fact that, from the first time she could make herself understood, two-year-old Jazz was so outspoken about being a girl trapped in the wrong body. Here's what Jazz said about this issue when she was interviewed by a teen magazine reporter:

> I feel that one of the biggest misconceptions centers around choice. Many think that transgender people are choosing a different gender, but this isn't true. I was assigned male at birth, but I've always been a girl. Just like any other girl, I've identified as female from as long as I can remember. [61]

To another magazine interviewer, Jazz added that being transgender is "something you're born with, and you realize that you're trapped in the wrong body. It's not like one day you're like, 'I want to be transgender!' " [81]

Marlo Mack, mom of a transgender girl, related her own experience grappling with this matter when her child was three-years-old. "I decided that enough was enough. I sat my child down, looked her in the eyes, and asked the question: 'Do you really want to be a girl?' Her reply was, 'I don't *want* to be a girl, Mama. I *am* a girl.' " [60] Renée Fabish, the parent of another trans child named Milla, stated on a YouTube video: "This is something that is in her genetic make-up. It hasn't been caused or encouraged by our parenting. It is not something she was talked *into*, and it is not something she can be talked *out of.*" [15]

The belief that parents are somehow responsible for their children's gender dysphoria, or that being transgender is a "choice," is pseudo psychology. However, a transgender individual's mental health *is* still a major concern. An article in *Wikipedia* explained that our society's negative response to these individuals puts them at an increased risk for stress, isolation, anxiety, hopelessness, poor self-esteem, and worse.[96] The trans community is probably the most misunderstood and ill-treated minority anywhere in the world.

"Transgender people are often harassed, socially excluded, subjected to discrimination, abuse, and violence, including murder." [96] One television documentary reported that, "Most trans children still live in the shadows, hiding from a world that sees them as freaks of nature. Many grow up hating their bodies and fall victim to high rates of depression, drug abuse and suicide." [94]

Why?

The psychological damage caused by people mistreating and rejecting transgender youth can be terrible, but it's even more significant if that individual's *own family* is not accepting, loving, and supportive. It is unfortunate this is often the case. 57 percent of transgender and gender-nonconforming people report experiencing rejection by their families. This leads to a dramatic increase in the incidence of homelessness, incarceration, and self-harm.[23]

Many times, parents of a transgender child erroneously think their youngster is just being rebellious, refusing to dress or act as expected for their gender. Damaging punishment often follows.[5] Or the parents may insist their child express themself in ways consistent with their birth-assigned sex, out of the mistaken belief this will protect that youth from discrimination. The unintended consequence is a child growing up experiencing numerous mental-health issues, such as self-loathing.[70]

It is quite common for parents to blame themselves for their youngster's gender variance, and to have feelings of guilt and shame about what other people might think. The parents' response may then be denial, or worse yet, they often reject their child and turn them out of the home. According to the Center for American Progress, (an independent, nonpartisan policy institute), while an estimated 5 to 10 percent of the total youth population are gay or trans, somewhere between 20 to 40 percent of all homeless youth are gay or transgender.[2]

Being unwanted greatly increases the risk of self-harm. A 2009 university study of LGBT youth experiencing a high degree of family rejection found them to be over eight times more likely to attempt suicide than those in accepting and supportive families.[32]

Discussing the remarkable difference in mental health between trans kids who *are* accepted by their families compared to those who are *rejected*, Jeanette Jennings shared this perspective with journalist Barbara Walters: "You know, I feel bad for those parents who can't give that acceptance to their children." Holding back her tears, Jeanette continued, "Some of them just can't put aside their own bigotry or feelings enough to say, it doesn't matter if you're gay, lesbian, transgender. Why should it matter? This is your child! "[94]

Leelah Alcorn, a 17-year-old trans kid, wrote a suicide note that addressed this phenomenon of parents not being accepting, supportive, or giving unconditional love to their children:

> When I was 14, I learned what transgender meant and cried of happiness. After 10 years of confusion, I finally understood who I was. I immediately told my mom, and she reacted extremely negatively, telling me that it was a phase, that I would never truly be a girl, that God doesn't make mistakes, that I am wrong. If you are reading this, parents, *please* don't tell this to your kids. Even if you are Christian or are against transgender people, don't ever say that to someone, especially your kid. That won't do anything but make them hate them self. That's exactly what it did to me.[57]

23

Soon after, Jazz wrote about Leelah. "She remains in my heart, and her voice should be heard to remind us all why we must treat each other with respect and love." [46]

As Jeanette told an ezine reporter, "It's a child's birthright to be loved unconditionally. Their parents need to remember that trans kids didn't ask to be born transgender. Parents need to put their own egos aside, and always put the well-being of their children first." [61] In the words of the Human Rights Campaign, "For some transgender youth, family support can be the difference between life and death." [34]

Once it was determined that Jazz was a transgender child, the Jennings were advised to be extra cautious how they dealt with this situation. Jeanette explained, "The doctors said, don't encourage it, but support it," and "follow her lead." [94] Greg added, "And we just keep listening to what she tells us." [87]

*****

No transgender or gender-variant child is the same, and they and their families each have unique challenges to overcome. Jazz's journey has had many of its own ups and downs, and has never been simple or easy. But once she was found to be transgender, the way onward has been relatively straight-forward.

Yet other trans or gender-nonconforming kids and their families often experience even more difficulties along their way. These children may take months or even years to unfold their own authentic gender identities, unlike Jazz, who has always known she is a girl. Combine that uncertainty with the lack of research-based information or diagnostic tools, and parents and families can have a very tough and confusing time figuring out how best to proceed.

Those who have successfully navigated this challenging path, such as the Jennings, share with other families that the best way ahead is to provide these kids with acceptance, shower them with unconditional love and support, and just be patient and follow their lead. Such an approach will greatly increase the likelihood that things really will get better. It is unfortunate so many transgender kids do not experience this kind of life at home.

*****

In a November 2011, Dr. Drew Pinsky television interview of Jazz and Jeanette, this exchange took place between Dr. Pinsky and Dr. Olson. They were discussing the psychological aspect of gender dysphoria:

> PINSKY: "I choke on the word *problem*, a *disorder*, because Jazz doesn't seem to be suffering, right?
> OLSON: That's correct.
> PINSKY: Doesn't there need to be some suffering associated with a disorder, right?
> OLSON: I think that's why people get disturbed that it's in the *DSM* (the professional mental health book) at all. It's called a

disorder, but it really is around the dysphoria (discontent) that exists when you are forced to live in a role that doesn't match your internal mental identity.[73] *

One reporter who interviewed Jazz expressed it this way: "Imagine how that must feel. To live inside a body that you really didn't want. To be labeled a gender that you know in your heart just isn't who you are."[84]

It is for these reasons that the term "Gender Identity *Disorder*" has been dropped from the latest edition of the *DSM* (2013), and replaced with the name "Gender *Dysphoria*" (discontent). This newer vocabulary reflects the more recent interpretation by mental health experts that a transgender patient's psychological distress is *not* a mental *disorder*. Rather, this anguish is based on the individual being extremely uncomfortable with the misalignment between their gender self-image (such as being a girl in their brain) compared to their physical body (such as having a boy body). And this pain is greatly intensified when a transgender person is subjected to discrimination and mistreatment.

Indeed, studies of transgender males in the Samoan culture discovered that little or no such psychological damage occurred to people there because that society is very accepting of boys and men who

---

*Some transgender activists believe that including gender dysphoria in the *DSM* is necessary to advocate for health insurance coverage of the medical treatment required by transgender patients. Others argue that gender dysphoria should just be reclassified as a medical issue instead of as a mental health concern, and that some insurance could still apply.

are more effeminate. In addition to male and female, their culture recognizes a third gender, "effeminate male." [96] Some very old cultures, including Native Americans, call this being "two-spirit." The notion that there are just two distinct genders, male and female, is a product of our modern western culture. Other cultures around the world, in times both ancient and contemporary, allow for a range of gender identities beyond that binary (two) gender model.

*****

Returning to the "why?" question, since it has clearly been shown that parents do *not* cause their children to be transgender, what is the source? Many medical specialists and researchers now believe the origin is likely biological in nature, such as a small alteration in the gene makeup of transgender peoples' brain structure and function.[94] (Genes guide how a baby's body develops.) Another theory is that an unusual exposure of babies to their mothers' hormone chemicals before birth might cause a mismatched gender to be imprinted onto the developing brains of trans children.[9/94]

These medical theories are bolstered by scientific research. According to Dr. Maddie Deutsch, clinical leader at the UC San Francisco Center of Excellence for Transgender Health, "There have been some brain imaging studies which suggest that trans people's brains are more like the 'opposite' birth sex. However there is certainly not any conclusive evidence" at this time.[11.1]

Another project is an ongoing, long-term University of Washington research study of transgender children ages three to 12 years old. This investigation tracks each child's responses to a series of gender-related assessments administered once each year over a ten-year period. Preliminary results show that the test responses of *trans girls* match those of *nontransgender female children*, and the same applies for the responses given by *trans boys* when compared to *nontransgender male children*.[83]

The findings of numerous scientific research studies are not as yet definitive. However, taken together, this growing body of evidence points in the direction of a genetic or other *physical* rather than *psychological* origin for being transgender. This is no more a "choice" that the critics claim than is being born with brown or blue eye color, or growing up to be short or tall, or left- or right-handed. Jazz's parents had nothing to do with her being transgender. Nor did the parents of any other LGBTQ child. It is just how some people are born.

Linda Thompson, once married to athlete and TV star Bruce Jenner, now Caitlyn Jenner, recently wrote an op-ed article in the *Huffington Post*. She was responding to Caitlyn's coming out on national television as a transgender person. Linda wrote:

> Being transgender is another part of the human condition that makes each individual unique, and something over which we have no control. We are who we are in the deepest recesses of our minds, hearts and identities.[89]

Chapter 4

Acceptance and Transition

With the gender dysphoria diagnosis confirmed, Greg Jennings' reaction was at first more denial. Looking back, he said about his feelings at that time, "Initially, I had difficulty accepting that my child was transgender." [84] Jeanette observed that Greg "was a little bit more resistant. He was at first not as cool with it." [28] Greg explained, "It was difficult. I wanted to try and have Jazz do things that were more intuitively *boy*." [28]

But as he thought more about what the professionals were saying, what his son was insisting, and what Jeanette was certain to be true and correct, Greg began to adjust his own attitudes and beliefs. "I had to get past any preconceived notion I had." [87]

> As time progressed, and I began to understand and gain some knowledge, at that point I realized her true essence was as a girl, and it was my responsibility as a dad to support her and love her unconditionally. I just knew it was what Jazz needed. She needed me to be strong and support her. [68]

The Jennings endeavored to learn more about transgender children. They were struck by the grim statistics associated with those children whose parents were in denial, did *not* allow the transition process to proceed, or outright rejected their trans kids.

Greg and Jeanette were especially concerned about the unusually high rate of suicide attempts among transgender youth and adults. Over the last few years, different surveys have found this rate to be 33 percent to 50 percent of all transgender people. That is many times greater than that of the general population. One of the most recent surveys was conducted by the National Gay and Lesbian Task Force and the National Center for Transgender Equality. Published in January 2014, this study found that 41 percent of all transgender people, both children and adults combined, attempt suicide in the United States each year. If counting just those under 18-years-old, this rate would likely be even higher, possibly approaching 50 percent. That compares to an estimated suicide-attempt rate of 1.6 percent to 4 percent of the general population.

More exact statistics are impossible to determine by these surveys because many transgender individuals are "stealth" (living in secret) or haven't yet worked out for themselves just what their gender identity is. A news article in the *Houston Chronicle* reported, "There are also no reliable statistics about the number of transgender boys and girls, in part because young children don't have the language to express themselves."[18]

In another newspaper article, Dr. Norman Spack, founder of a Boston clinic for transgender patients, stated, "We're talking about a population that has the highest rate of suicide attempts in the world, and it's strongly linked to nontreatment."[13] "With odds like that," commented Jeanette, "we weren't taking any chances with our child's life."[1] The Jennings readily came to the conclusion that, to put it bluntly, "We would rather have a healthy and happy daughter instead of a dead son." [21]

Jeanette and Greg decided to follow the experts' advice to recognize their child as being a girl.* Then they explained to their other three children what was occurring.[94] The young twin boys were understanding and agreeable. However, Ari, about eight-years-old, "had a rough time at the beginning," Jeanette now explains.[63] She was upset she would no longer be seen as the only girl, "the princess of the family." When her father explained to Ari about gender identity disorder and what a very difficult life this would be for the little child, Ari "started to cry, and said, 'I'm going to be the best big sister ever!' " Jeanette says ever since that day, Ari has lived up to her promise. "She has been supportive and awesome," [63] and is indeed the best sister anyone could ask for.

After that, the Jennings family began the slow and difficult process of accepting their little boy as really being a little girl.[94] "We came to the realization that, although Jazz was biologically a boy, we never truly had a son." [35]

It is interesting that years later, older sister Ari observed, "I never have thoughts like I miss my baby brother, because she never was my

---

*In a 2015 speech she gave, Jazz said about her parents, "At that time, they had no idea the adventure they were about to embark upon!"

baby brother. I just always saw her as a girl." [87] As a teen looking back, Jazz wrote, "My sister says I was always talking to her about my girl thoughts, and my girl dreams, and how one day I would be a beauuuutiful lady."[30] Sometimes kids are more perceptive than grownups. And Jazz did indeed grow up to be a beauuuutiful lady.

Going from expressing one gender, a boy, to another gender, a girl, is a long-term, step-by-step process known as *transitioning*. For the Jennings family, one big step along this journey was to invite their child to create a new girl name.[84] Since the age of three, she had been calling herself "Sparkles" because all things sparkly were very appealing.[44] So the idea of a name change was already in place. Her role model, big sister Ari, had just appeared as "Princess Jasmine" in the third-grade school play *Aladdin*. That inspired the now four-year-old to choose her new name "Jazz." [50 / 76]

The transition process was a very challenging time for the Jennings family. There were plenty of questions, concerns, and emotional roller coasters. Jeanette keeps a journal, and several years later she referred back to this period. Along with her child's name change, Jeanette packed away all his boy clothes, pictures, and videos. "I miss the boy, the baby boy. That child's gone." Like any parents experiencing the loss of a child, Jeanette and Greg mourned the loss of their son. Even years later, reading her journal entry to the interviewer brought Jeanette to tears. "But now there's a wonderful person that's with us, a sweet, loving daughter named Jazz." [94]

In addition to experiencing this sense of loss, Jeanette shared that there were other very emotional issues to face.

> It was an extremely painful and upsetting time for us. We weren't in denial, but we thought, how are we going to do this? Are we going to allow her to live as a girl, and switch that pronoun *he* to *she*? And we didn't know anybody else to ask for help. I'd searched all over the Internet for other parents, and *nobody* had transitioned that young. So I had sleepless nights. I talked to doctors. It was extremely scary. It was a grueling process, and we doubted ourselves. Are we doing the right thing? [68]

The Jennings were navigating in unknown territory, and confronting these issues all alone. "There are a lot of things we've confronted that we had no road map for," Greg observed. [40.1] One such issue, another significant step in transitioning, was allowing Jazz to wear girl's clothing, including dresses. At first, this was *only allowed at home*. When away from home, as well as at the preschool she was now attending, the Jennings chose for Jazz a more "gender-neutral look," with hair and clothes that were ambiguous. [94] Jeanette later acknowledged that she and Greg were simply not ready for Jazz to leave the house in girl clothes. [40.1] Besides, the preschool dress code wouldn't allow Jazz to wear a dress anyway. [28 / 94]

Not being permitted to be a girl outside home did not sit well with this very determined child. According to Jeanette, her kid just "wouldn't give up, was not happy until he could express himself as a girl" *both* inside their home *and in public.*[94] (Recall Dr. Olson's three gender-dysphoria key words: *insistent, consistent, and persistent.*) Jazz later shared that, as a four-year-old, it was confusing to be a girl at home, but be expected to appear as a different person to the world.[63] "Pretending I was a boy felt like telling a lie," Jazz wrote in her children's book.[30]

The situation got so bad, Jazz would lie on the floor by the front door, crying and screaming in a temper tantrum, refusing to leave the house dressed in boy's clothing.[63 / 68] This unhappiness and the daily struggles over how to appear at school and outside in public went on for months.[94]

To a television interviewer, Greg clarified his attitude about what outfits Jazz was allowed to wear in public:

> Well, there were occasions when she wanted to dress in girl clothes, and I said, 'No! I'm just simply not leaving the house with her dressed in girl clothes.' That was when she was younger, like three and four. I think by four, we started to move in the direction of *sometimes...*[68]

Years later, Jeanette explained more about her husband's response to Jazz asking to appear in public dressed as a girl:

> She wanted to go out in her dresses, and Greg felt slightly uncomfortable doing that. But he was always

very loving and embraced her and never tried to make her somebody she wasn't. He was just a little nervous about society being cruel and didn't want her to be made fun of.[80]

Jeanette said she and Greg compromised, allowing Jazz "to wear some girly clothes" to class,[35] which was acceptable to the cautious preschool director.[94] But dresses were still not allowed, nor was longer hair. When looking back at this situation some years later, Jazz observed, "This was the early 2000s. There was a lot of ignorance regarding trans people in general, but transgender preschoolers were unheard of." [44]

~Jazz Mergirl~

Chapter 5

Coming Out Party

And then something occurred that led to a life-changing decision. The turning point came in the spring of 2005, toward the end of the preschool year, when Jazz was four-and-a-half years old.[94] Jeanette had placed her in a dance class. When participating in a dance recital, Jazz desperately wanted to wear a tutu, just like all the other girls. But her parents were still not allowing their child to wear girl's clothes, especially dresses, outside home.

There is a family video taken at the recital showing a very unhappy-looking Jazz just standing there, barely moving, while the other children dance around her. She heaves a big, sorrowful sigh. Jeanette looks back on this episode as "a disaster." It is painful to view the video, about which Jeanette commented, "It was heartbreaking to watch. Really heartbreaking." [94]

Years later, when recalling this incident, Jeanette explained to a TV journalist that she at first thought her daughter was just being shy. But then Jeanette realized Jazz was actually very upset and angry. Standing frozen in place was her child's way of letting Mom know how she felt, and that this situation was devastating to her.[40.1] Thinking back, Jazz added, "Those were terrible times. Kids would make fun of me, and I was miserable. I just wanted to live as a girl all of the time, including at school." [36.1]

That was the wakeup call for the Jennings. It was time for their frustrated child to "come out" to the world as a girl. Jeanette shared with a newspaper reporter, "Once Jazz was four-and-a-half or five, Greg threw in the towel, and he knew we were going to have to let her transition. This was not going away." [80] In 2014, Jeanette wrote in an op-ed article, "It became clear to us Jazz's health and well-being were far more important than any binary (male and female) gender rules set forth by society." [35]

Jazz and her parents had been meeting with their gender therapist, Dr. Volker, to work on the many issues involved in making this transition. With the doctor's guidance, the process now moved forward, and a perfect "coming out" opportunity soon presented itself.

Jazz's fifth-birthday celebration, on October 16, 2005, was to be a huge pool party, with about 65 kids and their parents in attendance, and would feature a jumper and a very big waterslide. Jazz knew just what to do. She asked to wear her favorite one-piece, rainbow-colored girl's bathing suit. Jeanette thought this was fine because, after all, it was her daughter's special day, and she should be able to choose her own party outfit. Although Greg was still coming to terms with Jazz's transition, he agreed.[94]

Another family video captured this special occasion. Jeanette exclaimed, "She's beaming, she's so happy! You could just see on her face, her eyes were shining, a different light that she didn't always have." [64] Greg stated about this day, "That was the first time in front of everybody, *she* announced to the world that she was a girl." [21] He also noted that this "really was the first time we said to our friends, community, society, that we were going to allow Jazz to be Jazz. And it was an opportunity for Jazz to go out into the community and say, 'I am Jazz.' " [87]

Jazz remembers this as one of the happiest and most important days of her life. "It was the first time in public that I could be a girl. It was the first step in becoming the real me." [18] Thinking about all the challenges and difficulties they had experienced so far, Jeanette later commented, "But when we saw how happy she was, it made up for it." [68] In another interview, Jeanette stated, "There were no more haircuts after that day. That was it. Like, she's gonna be a girl." [40.1]

What took longer for the family was transitioning Jazz's pronoun from "he" to "she," which they finally started to do after that memorable birthday party.[36.1] This may not sound like a big deal, but pronouns, perhaps even more so than a name, are tied to a person's sense of self. Jazz's sense of self was as a girl (she), rather than as a boy (he). That's why the youngster had so vociferously corrected the gender therapist, Dr. Volker, "I'm a *girl*. I'm *she*," and why Jazz always reminded Jeanette, "No, Mommy, not good boy – good *girl*." [94]

~Jazz Mergirl~

Chapter 6

Social Transitioning

Following her fifth-birthday party, Jazz began what is known as *social transitioning*. In addition to her name and pronoun change, this meant starting to grow her hair out, getting her ears pierced, and wearing dresses outside the home.[94] Jazz fondly recalls the day (in late 2005 or early 2006) when she was first acknowledged by her family in public as a "full-fledged girl." She explained, "I went to Disney and wore a pink dress with Tinker Bell symbol on it. It was the happiest day of my life."[84]

Greg especially remembers one event away from their home, in March 2006, when Jazz wore special girl's clothing:

> It was an extremely hard day the first time I agreed to go outside the house and have Jazz dressed in a princess costume.[94] I went to the costume party. It was actually a Dad's Night only at the preschool, and there's all the dads, they have sons coming as super heroes, and Jazz was wearing a princess outfit. You know, it wasn't easy for me to go into a school and a room like that.[68]

This costume party was unlike the visit to Disney World, where the family was unremarkable in the vast crowds, and no one knew Jazz.

Dad's Night was a prominent appearance in the small preschool-classroom setting, where everyone *did* know the Jennings family. Quite a different experience for Greg and his newly-transitioning child. Greg kept his discomfort carefully hidden, and Jeanette now says how proud she is of her husband for doing what was best for Jazz, but most difficult for him. "That's one of the reasons I love him so much." [95] About this night, Greg concluded, "It was definitely one of the key points in time as it related to Jazz transitioning." [94]

In the meantime, the conservative preschool administrator had become a bit more cooperative about Jazz's unique situation and needs. The school director talked with Jeanette, and agreed to make a few concessions to the dress code. Jazz's longer hair style was allowed, as were flowery, sparkly clothes. While Jazz was pleased about these loosened rules, she was upset that, for her, dresses were still not permitted in preschool, although now allowed elsewhere outside home. This was when Jazz drew the picture of a tearful little girl that she would later show Barbara Walters on television. The girl is crying because her mother won't let her go to school in a dress.[94]

Dr. Olson, the adolescent children's specialist, commented about children wanting to express themselves according to their true gender identity:

> I think just the idea that people are transitioning or social transitioning in childhood is a really rare and new phenomenon. I personally think there are children who

are suffering so much and have so much social dysfunction that they drive a social transition themselves.[73]

Not everyone was supportive of the Jennings' decision to embrace their child's wishes. As their daughter's transition progressed into the public realm, the family realized that some people were pointing, whispering, and staring.[84] Jeanette recalled, "There were snickers, sneers, and gossiping." [35] She said, "You just have to look the other way. It's uncomfortable." [84]

But it was more than mere "tongue wagging." There was some very vocal community "pushback" about Jazz's appearance, and the family's use of female pronouns (she, her). Some prejudiced people not only were (and still are) critical of the social transitioning taking place, but added that this child was simply too little to know her own mind, and take such life-changing steps at so young an age.

In early 2006, in one of her first appearances on a transgender discussion panel, Jeanette addressed these criticisms:

> Some people say to me, "How can you let him walk around looking like that?" And I say, "Because that's what she picked out to wear today." We are doing something right because Jazz, rather than focusing on gender issues, lives a happy and well-adjusted life.[100]

While participating on the panel discussion, Jeanette also talked about criticisms she had heard regarding Jazz's transitioning at an early age. Jeanette rhetorically asked:

> How young is too young? I don't think it's ever too young
> to be who you are. At this point, what's the worst that
> could happen? If she changes her mind, we'll transition
> back. I'm trying to leave the door open, and I'm checking
> in with her feelings. I worry about today, and tomorrow
> I'll worry about tomorrow.[100]

"Jazz blossomed once permitted to transition, and hasn't wavered since," Greg Jennings says now. He went on to add, "She is a happy, well-adjusted child who enjoys life and embraces her individuality." [14]

Chapter 7

Kindergarten!

As the end of preschool approached, Jazz was excited about entering kindergarten, starting in August 2006, when she would be almost six-years-old. Following discussions with Dr. Volker, the gender therapist, Greg and Jeanette decided this was an ideal time to move forward with Jazz's transition.[100] In the record books, Jazz is believed to be, at that time, the youngest transitioning student ever enrolled in school.[9] She is quite a pioneer.

This turned out not to be the simple, straightforward procedure most parents experience when signing up their children for school. The Jennings were aware that their neighborhood elementary school's principal was quite a conservative administrator, something they had already experienced with the preschool director. According to Jeanette, she and Greg protected Jazz from the struggles that went on with this principal:

> What Jazz didn't see was behind the scenes stuff, because she was *so* happy she was finally allowed to go to school as a girl, and she was this happy kindergartner, but what she didn't know was that we had to *fight for her right* to attend kindergarten as a girl.[1]

Kindergarten!

As Jazz grew older, she began to learn about these difficulties from which her parents had shielded her. In a March 2015 speech to the Human Rights Campaign (HRC), Jazz shared some of the details about this situation:

> As kindergarten approached, my parents knew it would be harmful to my mental well-being to force me to conform, and start elementary school as a boy. In anticipation of resistance from the school administration, and to protect my rights, my parents called a meeting with the principal *months* before the 2006 school year was set to begin. They came in prepared with an attorney and my doctor by their sides.[44]
>
> To say the very-conservative school principal wasn't ready for me is *quite* an understatement. She couldn't wrap her mind around the idea of what she thought was a little boy attending her school as a girl. She was adamantly opposed to me starting school as a girl.[44]

Jeanette explained more about what was expected in order to proceed with the kindergarten enrollment. "The principal wanted Jazz to come in as a 'gender-neutral' child with no pronoun (she, her), and dress in neutral clothing, and sort of be an 'it' like Elmo."[1] And the school would use the boy birth name indicated on the birth certificate, which was required for school registration.

These requirements were definitely *not* acceptable. After much back-and-forth, an agreement was worked out so Jazz could attend kindergarten. She would be able to express her gender as female, teachers were to use her new name "Jazz" and the female pronouns "she" and "her," and most of the students would only know Jazz as a girl.[94]

Although their child was not present at the meeting, her parents knew how much she was looking forward to wearing a dress to school. But on top of everything else, the school administrator wanted Jazz to wear school-uniform pants or shorts.[44] The two sides compromised about the uniform policy, allowing Jazz to dress in "skorts" (a combination of skirt and shorts).

There was one last, important detail of the negotiations that Jazz shared about during her HRC speech:

> The only area we couldn't get the principal to budge on
> was the dreaded bathrooms. In my elementary school,
> each classroom had one gender-neutral bathroom with
> no locks. So basically anyone could walk in on you. How
> scary for a kid like me! [44]

In the end, the conservative administrator refused to permit Jazz to use any girl's bathroom on the school campus. She would just be allowed to use the unlocked unisex facility inside her classroom, or the nurse's restroom that sick or bleeding students messed up on a daily basis. About having to enter this unpleasant place, Jazz stated, "As you can imagine, I was horrified to use this infirmary restroom." [44] Although the Jennings didn't know it at the time, the struggle over the issue of the school bathrooms would go on for several years to come.

Meanwhile, on the first day of school, Jazz followed Mom to the kindergarten classroom, with Dad videotaping from behind. The video shows this cute little girl, with her hair grown out, dressed in a pretty pink outfit, and carrying a pink backpack and pink lunch bag.

Despite the difficulties with the school principal, kindergarten turned out to be a very good environment for Jazz to embark on this new chapter in her life. She got a fresh start as a girl, in a new school, with her new name, and a chance to make new friends, because she didn't know anyone in her class. Since the kindergarten restroom was unisex, as were the sports activities, gender was not so much a concern at that time. Jazz remembers, "Kindergarten was the happiest time for me. I was a girl officially." [87] She added, "I was finally the girl that I always thought myself as. It was the best time of my life."[1]

Chapter 8

Friends and Bullies

While Jazz flourished in kindergarten, she was still being sheltered from the struggles her parents were dealing with. This included negative feedback similar to all the criticism they heard during the preschool transition. Jeanette remembers she and Greg continued to have the same concerns they had all along: "Would she be bullied, would she be ostracized, would she have any friends. As parents we were always worried."[1] As it turned out, both would come true, the friends *and* the bullying.

Jazz has a small group of loyal friends who have been with her from preschool, and remain her "BFF's" to this day. They knew her as a boy, and say Jazz is the same person on the inside that they have always cared about and loved.[87] But in fifth grade, Jazz commented, "I don't have many friends at school," with the notable exception of an accepting group of students in her acting class that year.[87] Having a limited number of pals was an ongoing dilemma, made more difficult by Jazz's increasingly demanding schedule, which will be covered in another chapter.

An experience that helped change Jazz's outlook took place in the summer of 2014, during her vacation break following seventh grade. She attended a sleep-away camp on the east coast called Camp Aranu'tiq.[*] This is a safe and supportive place just for transgender and gender-nonconforming youth. According to Jazz, as related to a reporter for *17 Magazine*:

> I was anti-social in seventh grade, because I had trouble opening up to people. The following summer, I went to a camp for transgender teens where I made a lot of friends, and I entered eighth grade with more confidence. I found friends who accept me and realized they are the best support.[11]

After that experience, Jazz recalled, "For the first time, I invited girls over to the house, and we started hanging out more."[38] Besides summer camp, the good friendships Jazz has made have been at school, in team sports, and when attending transgender conferences. Several of these girls remain close. In her children's book *I Am Jazz*, she wrote, "The kids who get to know me usually want to be my friend. They say I'm one of the nicest girls at school."[30]

When Jazz was younger, Jeanette insisted on meeting the parents of new acquaintances before any home visits occurred. She would give them what she called "the talk" about her daughter being transgender, and invariably needed to explain what that means. It's still a topic poorly

---

[*]Aranu'tiq is an Inuit Indian word for "two-spirit," meaning a blend of male and female. The camp has a location in New Hampshire and one in Southern California.

understood by much of the public.[1] Some years ago Jeanette told an interviewer, "I don't want to send Jazz over to anybody's house unless they know the truth. Nor will I let an acquaintance walk into our house and spend time with Jazz, unless it's been explained to them."[94] Now that Jazz is older and more capable of discussing these issues with other kids by herself, she has taken over much of the responsibility for giving "the talk."

Jazz explained to one reporter, "When I get comfortable enough with a friend, I tell them that I have a girl brain and a boy body, and if they accept me, then they'll say, 'Oh well, you're still the same person, so of course I'll still be friends with you.' And if they don't, then they won't be my friends anymore."[1] She added, "I'm only friends with the people who will accept me for my true heart no matter what."[71]

Not all students treat Jazz with tolerance and respect. "Most kids are accepting, but others are mean," she says.[84] In her children's book, Jazz wrote, "Even today, there are kids who tease me, or call me by a boy name, or ignore me altogether. This makes me feel crummy."[30] Being a gracious and tactful person, Jazz chooses not to be much more specific. But to be blunt, it is not uncommon for this teen to be targeted both online and in person with obscenities and mouth-dropping, hate-filled epithets, and even death threats. These come from ignorant, bigoted people, often young men, but from older persons as well.

Jeanette Jennings added, "Trans kids are like other kids. But a lot of times, Jazz sits at lunch in school and people move away from her." [18] A news magazine reporter who talked with Jazz wrote:

> She's been called an 'it' and a 'freak,' and when she's called those things, Jazz tries to explain that being transgender is not a choice. 'It's just who we are,' she explains. Jazz tells kids that she doesn't have a disease, nor is she sick. She's just as normal as any other kid her age. 'Some people think that being transgender can be contagious, that's how crazy it is,' she states.[84] *

Speaking to Barbara Walters, Jazz discussed being subjected to discrimination: "Some people don't understand what the concept transgender means, and they think that I am weird, and that I shouldn't have the same rights as them just because of what's between my legs." [95]

In another interview, Jazz expressed her indignation about this prejudice: "It just doesn't make sense to me. I don't understand. Why can't I be a girl? That's how I feel, and that's it. It shouldn't matter about anything else." [68] In one of her responses to a YouTube comment, Jazz wrote what has become sort of a mantra for her: "What's most important is how I feel inside, because what's in between my legs doesn't define me. I define me."

---

* "Being gay is not a disorder. Being transgender is not a malady that requires a cure." US Surgeon General, April 10, 2015.

The news magazine reporter talked more with Jazz about her attitude when confronted with such prejudicial treatment:

> Jazz knows very well that she will continue to encounter discrimination. If her peaceful approach of explaining doesn't work, she has concluded that it's just best to walk away. 'Their opinions aren't important to me,' Jazz states. 'I understand that not everyone is going to understand, and I move on.' [84]

This teen is wise beyond her years. Perhaps Jazz is familiar with the *Serenity Prayer*. She certainly does follow its advice: "God, grant me the serenity to accept the things I cannot change, the courage to change the things I can, and the wisdom to know the difference."

In a 2009 television interview, Greg Jennings discussed his worry about Jazz being subjected to discrimination. He explained that since he and Jeanette knew what a challenging road lay ahead for Jazz, "We've tried to build as much self-esteem in Jazz as possible going into those future years, where we know it could be difficult." [28] Their parenting efforts certainly have paid off.

~Jazz Mergirl~

Chapter 9

TransKids Purple Rainbow

While Jazz was in the early stages of her transition, Jeanette and Greg continued doing research and consulting with a number of professionals about gender dysphoria in children. At that time (2005–2006), there were few books or online resources available on this topic, so Jeanette began reaching out on the Internet to other families of transgender youth. She is especially grateful to the Trans Families of Cleveland, with whom she continues to keep in touch. Jeanette also began attending transgender conferences to meet more experts and the parents of other transgender children. She never misses the annual Philadelphia Trans Health Conference.

As the Jennings learned more about people who are transgender, they became increasingly aware of the widespread struggles and suffering experienced by trans children and their families in the US and around the world. Added to that were insights Jeanette gained from attending and participating in those numerous conferences and other programs devoted to transgender issues. She also gained much perspective from her own child's difficulties before and during her transition.

Since Greg and Jeanette Jennings are such a caring and concerned couple, it was natural for them to begin thinking about ways they could be more involved in and supportive of the transgender community. They wanted to help improve the lives of trans kids everywhere. What the Jennings came up with was to establish a nonprofit organization dedicated to providing that help, and to advocating on behalf of the trans cause.

Launched in early 2007, the organization was named the TransKids Purple Rainbow Foundation. (TransKidsPurpleRainbow.org.) Jeanette is the president, Greg is a member of the board of directors, and a third member is a licensed mental-health counselor and gender specialist. Jazz is an "honorary co-founder." [53]

There are seven entries in the foundation's Mission Statement and Goals (see Appendix 6), but the most essential one states:

> TKPRF is committed to enhancing the future lives of TransKids by educating schools, peers, places of worship, the medical community, government bodies, and society in general, in an effort to seek fair and equal treatment of all trans youth.[53]

Another main goal of the foundation is raising funds to help homeless transgender kids, to fund other groups that sponsor camps and retreats for trans youth, and to subsidize research projects.[53] A third key foundation objective is to spread a message of tolerance, acceptance, and love by educating transgender youth and their parents, families, and friends.[53]

Jazz often expresses her appreciation for her caring family, saying she really doesn't know how she would have survived without them giving her their support and unconditional love. Jazz and her mom have met dozens of transgender kids who have been rejected by their families, and are homeless. They often drop out of school and engage in illegal activities to earn money for living expenses, and to help pay for their transition costs. Of her personal advocacy, Jeanette told Janet Mock, famed transgender journalist:

> These are the kids I really want to reach. I hear the stories, and I meet some of these young people, and they just cry, 'Why can't my mom be like you?' It's heartbreaking, and if I can just help one kid like that, it will be successful.[65]

> And then going beyond them by educating all the people that are on the fence, like they kind of know about this, but they really don't know, but they have an open mind. And finally, it'd be great to win over the people who look at us like crazy freaks.[65]

As of the time of this writing, Jeanette was working full-time on foundation business. Both Jeanette and Jazz are inundated with communications from near and far, including comments and requests that pour in on a daily basis via their various social media. In fact, Jeanette told listeners on one webcast that if they contact TKPR, she'd be the one reading all the emails and responding.[1]

Another task that takes up a lot of Jeanette's time is raising money to carry out TKPR's goals. Fundraising and donations are the lifeblood of the foundation's work.[*] TransKids Purple Rainbow successfully continues to fulfill its mission, and indications are it will keep expanding and thriving long into the future.

---

[*] Profits from *Jazz Mergirl* will go to support the foundation.

Chapter 10

My Secret Self

By 2006, Jeanette's involvement in numerous transgender-related conferences, panels, and Internet-based organizations was making her more known in the trans community. She was included in a news article about families with trans kids. When ABC Television began planning a Barbara Walters *20/20* special edition about transgender children, the producers came across this news article and contacted the Jennings.[76] They also spoke with a few other families raising transgender children.

Would these families agree to be interviewed for the television special? Many years later, a TV correspondent asked Jeanette about making this decision. She explained, "When ABC approached us, Greg was like, 'Absolutely not, definitely not!' It took 10 months of talking to the network for them to finally get us to say, okay, we'll do this."[40.1]

But it wasn't only Mom and Dad who needed to be on board with this choice. As a teen looking back, Jazz remembered talking with them about this decision, and how she too came to agree. "My parents told me that if I shared my story, I could maybe help other kids out there who might be struggling who are transgender. And once they told me, I knew it was the right thing to do."[40.1] Jazz was six-years-old at the time, the youngest identified transgender person to appear on TV.[9] Once again, she was a pioneer.

According to Barbara Walters, her staff not only negotiated with the parents. They also sought professional guidance from gender specialists to determine if the children would in any way be harmed by participating in such interviews and filming. After those 10 long months of talks, research, and negotiations, the program was finally green-lighted.[94] Titled "My Secret Self: A Story of Transgender Children," it was scheduled to air on April 27, 2007. The Jennings' segment with Barbara Walters was 16-minutes long, as they shared the one-hour program with two other families. Later that year, the documentary was nominated for an Emmy Award and won a GLAAD Media Award.

Jeanette said, "At first we were so scared to bring our story forward. But with the way Jazz was, she had such a positive message to give other children, and she was happy because we allowed her to transition." [65] She also observed, "You worry that other kids are going to go through this. Maybe if they saw Jazz's story, if their parents saw Jazz's story, it would help." [80] Greg and Jeanette's decision to allow their child to "come out" on national television "was the best thing we've ever done."[65]

Asked during a subsequent documentary interview what motivated the Jennings to participate in the televised program, Greg stated, "We feel that, by allowing you (the TV audience) into our home and into our lives, and seeing Jazz in her environment, doing the things she does on a daily basis, it will open peoples' hearts and understanding. It could make the world a better place."[28] Jeanette added, "We felt it was important to share our story with others, in the hope that we could raise awareness, educate others, increase tolerance, and bring positive change." [35]

Before finally agreeing to an appearance on the *20/20* show, there were a number of issues that the Jennings needed to figure out for themselves and take to the television producers for discussion.[*] Greg and Jeanette settled on four non-negotiable rules that they insist be followed. For the sake of privacy, and to protect Jazz, rule number one is that their real last name not be used.[35] That is why they have taken on the pseudonym "Jennings," and in the first *20/20* and one other documentary, Mom and Dad even used substitute first names (which they no longer do).

In addition, Jazz's birth name, which remains on her birth certificate and other official records, was kept confidential.[35] Family members sometimes use Jazz's original name. "They mostly call me Jazz, but sometimes they call me by my birth name." [50] Asked if that bothers her, Jazz responded, "No. It's because I don't care. If I really wanted them to stop, then they would, but my birth name is pretty neutral, so it's not too masculine." [50] The same applies for longtime friends who occasionally

---

[*] One idea the Jennings considered, and then dropped, was to have their faces blurred out on the TV program.[35]

use Jazz's original name that they always knew from preschool and the lower elementary school grades.[*]

For the most part, her friends, classmates, and teachers use Jazz's chosen name. A fifth-grade acting instructor commented that in class, many students called her "Jazz Matazz," [95] because she's so full of energy and enthusiasm.

Starting with the *20/20* "My Secret Self" documentary, the Jennings have been careful to only use the name "Jazz" during interviews or when on film. In fact, "Jazz Jennings" has come to be a "stage name," like many actors use. As mentioned, the purpose of having this public persona is for her privacy and protection. However, as explained in Chapter 1, Greg Jennings recently told a TV interviewer that Jazz's original birth name was Jaron.[40.1]

Jeanette shared more about the privacy issue when she spoke with a newspaper reporter in June 2015:

> 'Jennings' is our pseudonym, to sort of make life easier. We try to hide our real last name as much as possible. Our last name is a very long name. We found it easier at this point. She's known as Jazz Jennings. With the TV show (see Chapter 20), they're not going to tell anybody

---

[*] Worth noting, many in the trans community consider their birth name to be a "dead name," not to be mentioned.[19]

where we live. The TV show is not going to reference our true last name.[80]

The second non-negotiable rule is that the family's home location is to kept confidential, also for privacy and security concerns.[35] Then again, as Jazz grows older and more confident, and as the Jennings have become more comfortable in their public role, they have loosened this rule a bit. In an award-acceptance speech before the Equity Florida Gala, on November 16, 2014, Jazz explained how her public role is evolving in this regard:

> When our family decided to share our story in the media in 2006, we were all very scared. We made sure no one knew where we lived, for my personal protection. But now I'm happy to share with you that I'm an out and proud resident of South Florida! [51]

Rule number three is that TV interviews or articles are not to contain opposing viewpoints, like in a debate.[35] The Jennings contend that there is already enough ignorant and hate-filled speech directed toward transgender people, and they do not want to provide a forum for disseminating more of this misinformation or hatred.

But Jazz and Jeanette *do* reply to interviewers' questions about the transphobic beliefs and attitudes many people still hold. For example, during the Katie Couric Yahoo! News interview (October 2014), a brief news video was shown of angry (and ill-informed or closed-minded) parents complaining before a school board hearing. They were furious that the school district had enacted regulations protecting the equal rights of transgender students, especially the right to use the bathroom of their affirmed gender.

Both Jazz and Jeanette responded to this video in an articulate, knowledgeable, and confident manner.[9] One of their main goals is to educate the public, and spread their message of extending human rights, acceptance, and respect to all LGBTQ people, or anyone who differs from the mainstream.

The last of the four rules about filmed interviews and documentaries is that the Jennings be given an opportunity to review completed work before it is shown to the public.[35] This is to ensure that their privacy and security concerns have been met. However, as Jazz and her family appear more frequently on television and webcast programs, such a preview is not always possible. On the other hand, their request for confidentiality has been universally honored by the media.

Chapter 11

Ripple Effect

When asked by an interviewer what impact the *20/20* appearance had, Jazz responded that she really wasn't aware of the TV audience's reaction. Jeanette pointed out Jazz was only six-years-old at the time, too young to understand anything beyond her little world.[1]

> As she got older, I explained to her how she was making a difference and how things are really different from before she was born. She would get letters after she appeared on TV, and I'd read them to her from families and other kids, saying that she changed their lives, or even saved their lives, and she began to get an idea of how the media worked, and how she had an impact on the media, and was changing people's perceptions.[1]

> When we received letters from other parents thanking us for saving their children's lives, we knew we made the right decision. The emotions were overwhelming.[35]

And the impact goes on in a ripple effect. Since that first broadcast, Jeanette wrote:

Hearts and minds were opened to the hardships, discrimination, bullying, and extreme pain that trans youth experience on a daily basis. Parents of nonconforming youth all over the world realized that they were not alone. Suddenly, other kids began stepping out of their shadows to get accepted by their families and communities.[1]

In a reply to an interviewer's question, Jeanette had more to say about the changes she has noticed since Jazz's first television appearance:

What I've seen are more kids transitioning. When Jazz transitioned, I didn't know anyone that young who had transitioned, and after she came out, there were just dozens and dozens more kids coming out earlier. There's been a whole shift in the trans kids' movement. There was virtually nothing, and around the time we came out, all of these new programs started, and more kids were coming out. I've seen a huge change on the youth side of things.[1]

It can be quite moving to hear first-person accounts from some of these people whose lives have been transformed by the Jennings family's appearance on "My Secret Self." The Tylers are one such family affected by seeing the *20/20* program. In the movie *Trans*, Sarah Tyler, mother of four-year-old transgender Danann, explained that the

Jennings' documentary led them to greater understanding and acceptance of their child's challenging situation.

> One thing that helped was that our therapist had us watch the "My Secret Self" episode of *20/20* on YouTube, which focused on transgender youth. One of the stories, about a young girl, Jazz Jennings, could have been our own, right down to the fact that Jazz and Danann both love mermaids.[12] And immediately I realized, *that's my child!* We knew, okay, that's what our child is. We understand now. Clearly, Danann already knew who she was. It's just we were taking a long time to catch up.[4]

Another example of someone deeply affected by the "My Secret Self" broadcast is Katie Rain Hill, who wrote about this experience in her recently published autobiography, *Rethinking Normal.*[31] Ever since she was five-years-old, Katie had struggled to understand and cope with her feelings about gender identity, but got nowhere appealing to the adults in her life. By her early teens, she was desperate for answers and help, and began going on her mom's computer to do a surreptitious Google search: "I'm a boy, but I feel like a girl." Nothing of value ever showed up in response to these Internet inquiries.

Then one night in January 2008, Katie came across the transcript of the *20/20* program, "My Secret Self," in an article titled "I'm a Girl – Understanding Transgender Children."[21] For the first time, she read the "magic word transgender" and learned about Jazz Jennings' story. "As I read, I realized tears of joy were streaming down my face. There *was* someone like me. I was *not* alone." From this webpage, Google links led Katie to other related stories and videos available online.

Armed with the information and understanding she had acquired from the Internet, Katie was finally able to get through to her mother. That was something she had failed to accomplish over the last 10 years of her childhood. She even admitted to having wanted to kill herself, which is what Mrs. Hill had long feared.

When Katie showed her mother the article about Jazz Jennings, she watched her mom's face, "and I knew she was having the same reaction I'd had. Jazz sounded exactly like me. 'She's even obsessed with *The Little Mermaid*, just like you were,' " said Mrs. Hill.

Mrs. Hill read more online articles and viewed videos, "reading every word carefully, taking it all in." This was the turning point for both Katie and her mother. From then on, Mrs. Hill became her daughter's strongest ally, and fully supported Katie's subsequent transition.[31]

Jazz receives tons of emails and social media comments that say what a positive effect her story has had. They thank Jazz for being a role model. "I also get heartwarming letters from kids who tell me that I've changed their lives by sharing my story publicly." [61]

Here is one such comment posted to Jazz's YouTube *Q&A* video:

Jazz, I am a transgender girl who was born trapped in a male body. I was so scared to tell my parents that I hid it for years, and now because I saw your videos, you gave me the courage to tell them, and now I am happy and starting the transition. All people should accept you for who you and I are. Thank you for helping me get the courage. I had gone through puberty in the wrong body and am now 17, and I wish I had told my parents when I was younger.[42]

Another YouTube follower wrote:

Hi Jazz. In three days I turn 50. For the first 47 years of my life I lived what I call a life of survival. I did everything as manly as possible and acted as manly as possible because I felt I needed to do that in order to survive. Then I watched some interviews with you and your family, and I sat and cried for the longest time. Seeing you as a little girl reminded me so much of myself at that age. I saw the me that could have been, but never was. It gave me hope and inspiration.

Within a few months of seeing those interviews, I was able to come out to my closest friends and family. Then on August 1, two years ago, I began living my life as I should have from the beginning. I guess what I'm trying to do here is to say, "Thank you." Because of all of the people in the world, you truly saved my life just because you exist. I don't use the term "saved my life" lightly. In the truest sense of the word, you saved my life, and you never even knew it. So, not only does my heart go out to you and your family, but my thanks as well. Thank you.[42]

Jazz replies to such comments by saying this is exactly what she hopes to accomplish by appearing in the media, that she is very honored she can be of help to other people, and that being a part of such positive change makes her feel really pleased and happy.

In a June 2012 award acceptance speech before one thousand people, Jazz added more details about the effect the "My Secret Self" documentary had:

When my family and I first decided to share our story publicly, we were all very nervous. At the time, there were no young trans kids in the media. But after we shared our story on *20/20* with Barbara Walters, hundreds of other children and *their* families realized they were not alone. Families started to listen to youth who were gender nonconforming, and more kids like me were allowed to be true to themselves. It is so rewarding to inspire other children, because, let's face it, we are just kids, and *all* kids deserve to be happy.[39]

One interviewer asked Jazz how she manages to speak before such large groups that often include celebrities. She explained her inspiration this way: "It's all dedicated to encouraging other kids to be themselves, and step out of their shadows. I do it just to create change and make a difference. That's the only reason I make these appearances. That's what gets me through it."[1] In another context, Jazz once wrote, "I just think about how it will impact others. It's not about me." [50] As hundreds of thank-you comments, emails, and letters have shown, Jazz is indeed creating change and making a huge difference in so many lives.

The ripple effect has left its mark beyond the LGBT community at large. It has impacted the Jennings family as well. Jeanette commented on this in a podcast interview in May 2014:

> As a family, it's made us more in touch with people's feelings, and also more accepting of the world in general. My kids are all bleeding hearts. They all reach out to the kid that's being bullied, or the kid that's sitting alone in the lunchroom. They are very, very compassionate as a result of the discrimination they've seen. They've seen Jazz go through a lot also, with kids making fun of her. It's made us all better people having Jazz in our life.[54]

On a webcast discussion along with Jazz, Jeanette stated, "I'm truly honored to be her mother. She has made us, our family, and really the world, a better place for her being here." [63]

~Jazz Mergirl~

Chapter 12

First Grade Frustrations

Although kindergarten had proven to be a wonderful experience for Jazz, things changed when she moved on to first grade and was required to attend classes and activities in other locations on the school campus. The principal still would not allow her to use the girl's restroom. Jazz just hated it whenever she had to go into the nurse's bathroom that had been used by students who were vomiting or bleeding.[44/84] In a keynote speech Jazz gave in 2015, she revealed more details about this situation:

> As a result, I would hold my bladder, and I often had accidents. I'd also sneak into the girl's bathroom when I thought no one would notice. Until the day I got caught in second grade. I was reprimanded by the school librarian. I was told that I'd be sent to the principal if I tried to sneak in again. Can you imagine getting in trouble for using the bathroom? [44]

To Jazz, this state of affairs was an outrage and an affront to her dignity and identity. At age nine, in a YouTube video entitled *Message to Obama*, Jazz expressed her indignation at not being treated equally: "I got in trouble for using the girl's bathroom, and I should have the right to *use that bathroom*! I'm not different from anybody else, and I can lock the door and make sure they don't walk in!" [36.1]

By the time Jazz entered fifth grade in August 2011, conditions had improved a great deal. That year, the elementary school got a new, much more reasonable and understanding principal. About the same time, the school board had taken action to bring the district code into conformity with regulations issued by the Civil Rights Division of the US Department of Education. The board passed new school district policies that prohibited discrimination against LGBTQ students.[*]

Then the principal agreed to change Jazz's school records, which now designate her as a female entitled to use the girl's restrooms.[84] Jeanette said she and Jazz were very pleased with the much more accommodating manner in which they were being treated by school administrators.[87] And Jeanette was especially glad that the next year, Jazz would be able to enroll in middle school as a girl, no questions asked.[84]

When she entered middle school in August 2012, Jazz found the school staff very supportive and understanding. She stated, "My wonderful principal made it clear that I'd always be treated like all the other girls. I use the girl's bathroom, and even the locker rooms, and I wear what all the other girls wear." [44] One potential problem that was worked out before school started involved the changing room. In order

---

[*] Title IX of the federal education law prohibits discrimination against students on the basis of sex, gender identity, or sexual orientation.

to avoid difficulties and protect her privacy, Jazz changes uniforms in the adjacent girl's restroom, not in the locker room itself.

"Mr. L," the dean of student discipline, was always on top of any issues that did arise. Jazz explained, "Every now and then there will be that one kid who gives me a rough time, and teases me behind my back. And then they are sent to Mr. L's office. You do not *ever* want to go to Mr. L's office!"[44] Jazz's middle-school experience was a huge improvement from the time when she wasn't even permitted to use the girl's room in elementary school.

~Jazz Mergirl~

Chapter 13

Sports: Setbacks and Success

At the same time the school restroom problem was still going on, another battle over rules and regulations was developing. This time it involved athletics. "I love to play sports," Jazz told an e-journalist. "I've been an active athlete for as long as I can remember." [93] So, at a young age she eagerly joined the local Youth Soccer League division for five- to eight-year-old girls. Jazz's dad and twin brothers had helped coach her before that, and she became a very good player, quick and agile.

However, in September 2009, when Jazz was still eight, the state Youth Soccer Association banned her from participating in girl's travel soccer games. This action was most likely in response to parent complaints, and the reason cited was that being a biological male gave Jazz an unfair benefit (even though she was the smallest kid on the team). She recalled:

> It was devastating. I didn't understand. The state soccer league thought since I was born a boy, I had an advantage, even though I didn't at all. Many of the other girls were bigger than me. I was a dainty child. It was ridiculous. [84]

Jeanette added, "They said she could play with the boys if she wanted to, but you're not welcome to play with the girls."[1] Jazz told one sports reporter that she actually *did* try participating with the boys.

> But it was a disaster. It made me feel depressed, and I couldn't enjoy the game I love. I didn't want to quit soccer, so I decided to practice with the girls and face the injustice of being forced to sit out the games. I felt like I was being bullied. It was terrible and painful.[93]

For over two years, while Jazz continued to practice with her girl's team, she was only permitted to watch from the sidelines during actual games. Needless to say, she was extremely disappointed, sad, and angered, which could readily be seen by the look on her face in game videos from that time. In October 2011, while holding back tears of frustration and anger, Jazz told a TV interviewer, "It's very upsetting 'cause if I go to the game to support my team, I know that I'm not going to play, and I'm just sitting on the bench." [87]

Usually Greg Jennings is a pretty self-contained guy who doesn't readily reveal his feelings in public. But on a TV documentary titled *I Am Jazz*, he choked up while reading an email that he had sent to the soccer board. The email message was a plea for the board to allow Jazz to play travel games with her girl's soccer team. "Your decision has taken away a piece of her heart, and of her parents." [87]

"It was very touching, and I cried," Jazz said of her father's poignant moment in the film. "That was the part that got me, and when people see it, I think they'll feel that I deserve to play girl's soccer." [65]

One thing Jazz's dad included in his email was a quote of Jazz's response when informed she couldn't play: "Why don't you tell them that just because I'm a little different doesn't mean I should *not* have the right to play with my team. Tell them it's not fair!" [87] Greg went on to say, "We promised her that we would do everything we could to help have policies changed so that children like Jazz everywhere should never have to go through what she has gone through." [87]

Picking which legal battles to fight, the Jennings decided to put the elementary-school bathroom issue on hold to focus on the soccer ban. They undertook what turned out to be a two-year series of appeals to local, state, and regional youth soccer officials. Greg, who is an attorney, joined by the National Center for Lesbian Rights (NCLR), used his legal skills to pursue the case all the way up to the US Soccer Federation (USSF) in Chicago. It seems clear that this was another case of gender discrimination, like the girl's restroom situation.

However, the case did not end up in court over these legal issues.[*] In December 2011, the USSF Board of Directors ordered the state youth

---

[*]US Title IX civil-rights provisions only apply to schools receiving federal funds, which would not apply to the privately-funded soccer association. There were other legal protections that perhaps could have come into play.

soccer organization allow Jazz to participate in girl's-league travel games.[14] The Jennings were ecstatic. Recalls Jazz, "My family and I celebrated! It was great to be back on the field playing with my friends as the girl that I am." [93]

But this case was not about Jazz alone. The US Soccer Federation went on to establish a committee to investigate transgender issues in recreational soccer association teams. This group carried out extensive research and hearings, including an all-day session with the NCLR and their sports project director Helen Carroll.[99]

The committee chair, Dr. Contiguglia, a former president of the USSF, said: "As a physician, having had transgender patients, this was all pretty clear to me. There were some misperceptions that someone born a male would have an unfair competitive advantage playing against girls. But that's not true." Being the coach of an under-13 boy's team, Contiguglia regularly sees girls the same age who are "six inches taller than our guys." [99]

The committee ultimately recommended a number of revisions to the federation's rules, which were almost unanimously voted into place by the Board of Directors. Quoting Dr. Contiguglia, these new regulations can be summed up in a few simple words: "We don't discriminate. We accept who you say you are, so long as you follow the rules." [99] The case that the Jennings pioneered led to the enactment of this new national Soccer Federation policy that allows anyone to participate in the soccer league team of their self-affirmed gender. This is a victory that Jazz and her parents are particularly proud of.

The USSF was the first national sports governing authority to institute such a welcoming policy.[99] The guidelines establish a routine procedure for soccer players to declare their team-gender preference by showing a government-issued document such as a passport or driver's license, or by presenting a doctor's or therapist's letter. Any challenge to a player's gender identity is immediately heard before a USSF-appointed committee. This eliminates the need to go through a tedious and time-consuming local, state, and regional appeals process like the Jennings family experienced.[99]

It is unfortunate that these new rules do not apply to members of our own national soccer team. At this time, the international soccer organizations that the USSF belongs to (the IOC and FIFA) have a different set of regulations that must be followed.[99]

A few months after the Soccer Federation's decision, there was more good sports-related news when Jazz enrolled in the middle school. This school is part of a larger high school campus. That automatically brings the entire sports program under the auspices of the state high school athletic-league regulations. These include a rule that transgender students can play with the team that matches their affirmed-gender identity.[93]

As a result, Jazz felt free and welcomed to participate in a number of other sports, in addition to being a forward on the school's girl soccer team. In eighth grade, she joined the middle school girl's cross-country track team. Jazz now runs a respectable, middle-of-the-pack, 14-minute pace on the mile-and-a-half event, and about 17 minutes for the 3K run.

Jazz was very pleased with all these new opportunities in school sports. She shared her feelings in an interview with a sportswriter:

> My happiest day was when I found out that I was allowed to play varsity girl's tennis, or any other high school sport, because my state has a trans-inclusive policy. There was a process involved, but it worked with very little delay. It was a much better experience than having to fight to create a policy, as we did with the youth soccer league. I lost most of my tennis matches, because it was my first year, but I still loved playing with the team and my friends.[93]

Notice that Jazz said her tennis standings were those of a beginner. It will be typical of Jazz to keep working on her tennis skills until she plays up to her potential. Something else that really pleases Jazz is the positive atmosphere in which she now plays. "Almost all of my current teammates, their parents, and my coaches, are all very supportive." [93]

Chapter 14
Questions and Concerns

Following the broadcast of "My Secret Self," the Jennings family was asked to participate in numerous other television documentaries and magazine and newspaper interviews. As they did so, additional questions and concerns came up that needed to be addressed, beyond the four main rules worked out for that first 2007 ABC *20/20* appearance. (Those rules were: to keep their name and location private, not to engage in debates, and if possible, to preview the final version of news articles and videos.)

"With each media proposal came decisions about how much of our lives to expose." Jeanette wrote that she and Greg "spent many nights debating and sometimes disagreeing, but ultimately we wouldn't participate in any projects unless we both agreed on the parameters." [35]

For instance, they had to decide how much information to disclose about Jazz's medical treatment. The Jennings have been surprisingly open and frank about this subject. They have even allowed TV cameras into the doctors' examination rooms and granted permission for the documentarians to interview Jazz's medical team. That has to take a lot of courage, especially from Jazz. While most people would consider this an invasion of their privacy, the Jennings family made these concessions because they are *so* determined to enlighten and educate the public and to effect change.

Initially, however, there were some medical subjects off-limits to interviewers. One such topic was about *gender confirmation surgery* (SRS) discussed in a later chapter. Jazz is too young for that, and besides, she's entitled to at least some privacy. Even so, as Jazz got older and better able to speak for herself, that confidentiality rule has been substantially modified.

As a young teenager, Jazz has of late been quite candid and brave by openly sharing some very personal issues related to being trans, including concerns about her body image. Also, in a July 2015 Fusion TV interview with Alicia Menendez, Jazz talked about the daily medication regimen she follows, and about the chemical effect her body will experience if she does undergo the SRS procedure. Giving up a significant measure of her privacy is a price Jazz says she is willing to pay to increase public understanding and acceptance of those in the transgender community, and to help other trans kids feel more supported.

Another issue that arose concerning interviews is whether or not to share information on the subject of Jazz's *sexual orientation* (*sexual identity*). That means, "Who is the person attracted to?" Boys, girls, both, or none at all? As children move from adolescence, through their teen years, and on into adulthood, they go through a process of unfolding their individual sense of self, including their sexuality. For Jazz, like all other youths, it's a time of exploration and discovery. With this in mind, her parents have wisely decided to give Jazz the room she needs to work out for herself just what is her sexual orientation.

In the 2013 documentary "Listening to Jazz" on *20/20*, [95] and again in an August 2014 magazine article,[84] Jazz stated without hesitation that "I am attracted to boys." But by 2015, Jazz's thinking had evolved, and she acknowledged, "For me, my sexuality, I'm not really sure." [40.1] Now she relates to the concept of being *pansexual*, which, Jazz wrote, "means I love someone for who they are regardless of gender or sexuality." [42] "I'm going to go with the flow and wait until I find that special someone who looks at me for who I am on the inside." [40.1]

Jazz has been thinking about this for some time. When she was just 11, Barbara Walters asked her, "Are you afraid that you might not have dates with boys?" to which Jazz replied, "I am a little bit, but if any of the boys decline me because of my situation, then I just know they are not right for me at all." [95] *

Jeanette was also concerned that boys might not want to date Jazz. A few years later, when her daughter was 14 and in middle school, a TV journalist once again brought up the dating question. Jeanette revealed that Jazz now gets tons of requests via social media and email, from tweens and teen boys her age. Their messages ask for dates, or contain love letters, and even marriage proposals.[68 / 77.1]

---

*Jazz did have a boyfriend for a very brief time in fifth grade.[50]

But having boys reject her still troubles Jazz. What she really would like right now is to have some friends who are boys, not necessarily a boyfriend.[40.1] Not long ago, Jazz responded to one online comment by writing, "A lot of boys at school avoid me because they don't understand." [50] When someone countered that lots of boys show their interest for her on social media, Jazz wrote back:

> No boys *at school* like me. It's easier to say online. But in person, if anyone likes me, they have the chance of being bullied or teased by being called 'gay,' cuz they like another 'boy' (me). So it's either that they hide it, or they say I'm just really ugly.[50]

In June 2015, Jazz joked with her friends that she thought they were going "boy crazy." [40.1] But as for herself, she told a TV interviewer, "I'm not crazy about dating a lot right now because there's just so much going on, and I don't have time for a boyfriend or a girlfriend or whatever." [80] She told another journalist that she had no intention of dating until sometime in high school, "just to make my life a little easier." [63] But then, as ninth grade approached in August 2015, and Jazz saw her friends beginning to go out with boys, she began thinking more about that for herself too.[40.1] It's a confusing situation, but Jazz will work it out in time.

When that time does come, Jazz and her parents have already discussed how complicated dating may be for her, and that she must be honest about who she is.[84] "There have been other transgender people who have been murdered because they didn't tell the people they were dating that they were transgender," Jazz says. "So I know I'll have to be careful. It doesn't make me nervous, but it makes me cautious." [84]

One more important decision the Jennings needed to make concerning future interviews was about discussing religion. Greg and Jeanette are well aware that public discourse regarding LGBTQ issues is already fraught with a heavy dose of religion-based criticism and controversy. The Jennings are an observant family. However, they have concluded that bringing religion into the conversation would only become a distraction to their mission of expanding public understanding, acceptance, and support of transgender persons. As a result, the family has avoided publicly conversing about faith.

The one time Jazz *has* mentioned religion was in her YouTube *Letter to the World*:

> When some people say we don't appreciate God's creation or argue that the Bible doesn't say LGBTQ people are ethical, I get confused. Didn't He want us to spread love and kindness to all? [41]

~Jazz Mergirl~

Chapter 15

Filmed Appearances, 2008 – 2011

Over the years, as Jazz and the Jennings have become more known, they have often appeared on screen. But being recorded began way before such prominence. Greg and Jeanette have long been active videographers, taking lots of family videos. For Jazz, that began in the delivery room the day she was born. In addition to the videos, Jeanette has taken loads of photographs, too. All of these images provide an archive of family pictures that frequently are used to enhance interviews in which the Jennings appear.

Eventually Jeanette started to experiment with a YouTube channel (GnetLuvsGreg). Jazz was seven-and-a-half when she appeared for the first time on a YouTube video, filmed and edited by her mom. It was uploaded in June 2008. In the brief clip, Jazz says about being transgender that, "It's okay to be different because it just matters who you are. It just matters if you're having a good time, and you like who you are." [36]

The posted video received many comments that fell into four main categories: those that were appreciative and supportive, a number that posed questions, some that were religion-based and critical in nature, and finally, comments expressing hate and threats. To this day, those are the four main types of remarks that continue to be posted on Jazz's videos and other social media.

After the 2007 ABC "My Secret Self" program, it wasn't until April 2009, when Jazz was eight-and-a-half, that the Jennings were featured on another televised news program. This time it was for an ABC affiliate in Australia, which used the same title, "My Secret Self," on the Australian version of the *60 Minutes* TV series. The host, Liz Hayes, traveled to the United States to visit Jazz's family. The nine-minute segment's format was similar to the Barbara Walters *20/20* interview, but by now Jazz was older, less shy, more self-assured, and seemed to be growing happier.[28]

There was a long interval of two-and-a-half years until the Jennings once again agreed to be interviewed, and they made up for lost time with a flurry of TV appearances. The first of these programs, shown in mid-November 2011, was a nine-minute television interview with Rosie O'Donnell on her Oprah Winfrey Network (OWN) program. This appearance was arranged to publicize an upcoming one-hour OWN television documentary titled *I Am Jazz, A Family in Transition*.[87] It was scheduled to air one week later. After being introduced, Jeanette shared with Rosie that she and Greg "took a long time" to decide if they were willing to do the OWN documentary.[69]

Jazz, on the other hand, was enthusiastic from the beginning. She told Rosie, "I was really excited because I wanted to share my story with the world, so they can understand how it is to be transgender." [69] On television, Jazz's mature, confident, self-assured style belied her age, coming off as being much older than a child who had just turned 11 the month before.

After talking for a few minutes about questions Rosie had, the host asked Jazz for her thoughts concerning Chaz Bono on *Dancing with the Stars*. "He's kind of like my hero, 'cause he's really brave to come out with his story." Jazz and Jeanette were surprised when Rosie brought out Chaz, a transgender role model Jazz was very pleased to meet. They all chatted together briefly before the commercial break, and then the Jennings' segment ended.[69]

Later on, in November 2011, just days before the OWN *I Am Jazz* program was to be broadcast, Jazz and Jeanette visited by videophone with the *Dr. Drew on Call* show on the HLN channel. (A portion of the transcript is included in Chapter 4.) Their appearance was another opportunity to publicize the upcoming OWN documentary.

This segment of the *Dr. Drew* program was titled "A Child in Transition," and included Dr. Johanna Olson, the physician from Los Angeles Children's Hospital who specializes in treating youth with gender dysphoria. Many of the questions Dr. Drew asked Jeanette, Jazz, and Dr. Olson were similar to those posed in previous interviews. However, some topics discussed were, not surprisingly, more medical in nature, and are incorporated elsewhere throughout this book.[73]

Finally came time for viewers to see *I Am Jazz: A Family in Transition*, which OWN broadcast on Sunday night, November 27, 2011. On *The Rosie Show*, Jeanette had stated she and Greg weren't very enthusiastic about undertaking another big project, nor were they comfortable once again going public on one more in-depth TV documentary.[87] While the *20/20* "My Secret Self" episode was shared with the stories of two other families, this new film would be a one-hour special just about the Jennings, and would involve an extended filming schedule. It took several weeks for the producers of the Figure 8 Films Company to convince Jazz's parents to do the show.

As Jeanette had anticipated, this was the family's biggest project ever, with a production crew filming the Jennings family over a two-week period in late September and early October 2011. The approach used by the documentary's director, Jen Stocks, was to keep the interviewer off camera, and later edit out all of the questions. What remained were just the "first-person" responses of Jazz, her family, doctor, friends, and so forth. (In all the other Jennings interviews, the reporter or journalist, such as Barbara Walters, was present on camera.)

A distinctive feature of this documentary was that *all* the narration was provided by the Jennings themselves, who spoke about and gave context to every filmed sequence. Each family member got to do their share of narrating, which made the program more personal and appealing to the television audience. Interwoven among all the documentary's scenes were the numerous family photos and videos that the Jennings had taken over the years. Skilled editing brought all the pieces together to yield an engaging, informative, and heartwarming film.

Having a camera crew tag along for two weeks was a challenging experience. One film sequence began in the pre-dawn hours, cameras rolling in the dark as bedroom lights first came on. Filming didn't stop until Greg drove the four kids off to school. Another segment, filmed at night, was of the twins' flag football game, with Dad in his coaching role, and the rest of the family cheering along. As narrator, Greg explained that the Jennings are a very close-knit family, and always support each other by attending whatever activities one of them participates in.

One very special filmed sequence showed Jazz in the family pool, swimming in her mermaid tail. An underwater camera caught her gracefully gliding along below the surface. This filmed piece was selected as the documentary's mesmerizing introductory scene, and it was accompanied by the magical instrumental song *Mermaid,* which had just been released earlier that year. [*]

During those two weeks of filming, there were three other important events that provided more interesting opportunities for the documentary. The first of these was having the film crew go along with Jeanette and Jazz as they participated in a transgender panel discussion before an audience of college students. The conversation was moderated by Dr. Volker, Jazz's therapist, who taught classes at that school.

---

[*]*Mermaid* by Amber Music on the Blue Sky Project album, 2011.

By this time, Jazz was quite used to participating with her mom in various discussion groups. When Jazz was only eight or nine years old, Jeanette invited her to come along to one meeting, and she took right to it. According to Jeanette, people just love her. "She's charming, and she's got charisma, and she's so cute!" [87] In addition, Jazz is articulate, thoughtful, and poised in front of an audience. In fact, Jazz has stated that she enjoys making these appearances, and actually likes the attention.[73] "I love inspiring people when I go on the panels. And I love when they say that I'm doing the right thing." [87]

Most important, Jazz is always willing to share her story and spread the Jennings' message of understanding, acceptance, and equality for transgender people and anyone else who is unique. At this time, in the medical, therapy, and child welfare fields, there is a significant lack of knowledge and expertise about gender dysphoria. As a result, transgender panel discussions and symposia are invaluable in spreading awareness and understanding into the professional world.

At the panel discussion with Dr. Volker, the other participants were much older transgender people, in their 40s and 50s. None of them had transitioned as a young person, like Jazz has done. And unlike her, all went through "puberty" (growing into a man or woman) in their birth-assigned gender. She listened to them tell stories of such pain and suffering, being forced to live in bodies that never matched their gender identities until much later in life.

The camera zoomed in on Jazz, who was listening intently, and it was plain to see on her downcast face a look of deep sadness. She is a very thoughtful and compassionate person, far beyond her years. The camera also caught the look on Jeanette's face as she watched Jazz's reaction. Jeanette knew exactly what her daughter was thinking. This was one of the documentary's most poignant scenes.

But there were lighthearted moments as well, such as when a student inquired about the possibility of Jazz taking medication to become more feminine looking, and Jazz blurted out, "I want boobs!" Everyone laughed.[87]

All of the adult panelists seemed to agree that, in contrast to the time when they were young, there is now much more hope and opportunity for transgender kids like Jazz to find happiness early on. In this same regard, Aiden Key of Gender Diversity recently made a most profound observation. Speaking to a gathering of parents about their transgender youth, part of *Generation Z*, he said: "The world is watching your children. They are the first generation of kids to be allowed to live in another gender. Your children are making history." [60]

During the panel discussion, Jazz revealed that the next day, she and her parents were scheduled to meet with a medical specialist to discuss *her own* impending puberty. This was another filming opportunity for the OWN cameras. As was previously mentioned, the Jennings have been remarkably candid and generous in sharing with documentarians about Jazz's medical treatment. Thus it was not a surprise to see the camera crew follow right along into the exam room.[87] More about this momentous visit with the doctor will be shared in the next chapter.

The closing scenes in *I Am Jazz* were filmed around Jazz's 11th–birthday surprise party. The celebration featured a mermaid-themed cake, lots of presents, and having fun with longtime friends from preschool days.

As the documentary drew to a close, Jazz had the final say: "For anyone out there who is transgender and they are scared to step out of their shadows, it's okay to be different and be who you are. Just know that you're special, and love yourself." [87]

Chapter 16

The Blockers

2011 was an exceedingly busy year for Jazz. Besides all of the TV interviews, another significant life event occurred in October, when she turned 11. One year before, Jazz had first met with her pediatric endocrinologist (a children's doctor who specializes in body chemistry) and was returning for her annual checkup.* The doctor asked Jazz several questions, and then she conducted a physical exam that determined Jazz was just entering *puberty*. This is the period in life when the brain signals the body to produce chemicals that start to change a boy into becoming a man, and a girl into a woman.[87] Once these changes are complete, they are not reversible (except by costly and invasive surgical procedures).

The physician told the Jennings that Jazz had about six more months before her body would begin developing masculine characteristics. By then, a decision should be made regarding administering a special puberty-blocking medication to prevent those bodily changes from occurring. Jazz was distressed not to begin taking these drugs immediately. Her parents needed time to do some research,

---

* The OWN *I Am Jazz* documentary television crew was present for a portion of the appointment.

think over the choices, and investigate what kind of financial assistance the family's insurance company would provide for such treatment.[87]

Although their schoolmates are usually pleased and proud to be growing up, youth with gender dysphoria are, by definition, very unhappy and upset about beginning puberty. Most have never felt comfortable in their bodies to begin with, and this feeling is multiplied with the onset of these physical changes. Trans girls like Jazz are often very distraught with the thought of developing male physical characteristics, like a larger, heavier body with wider shoulders, larger hands, feet, and thighs, to say nothing of larger genitals. Trans boys, of course, don't like the idea of growing breasts and wider hips, having their bodies grow less in stature and weight, and beginning their periods.[96]

Jazz had been dreading entering puberty, where she would develop other manly features as well, such as an Adam's apple and a deeper voice, and the beginnings of facial and other coarse body hair. In fact, over the previous two or three years, she had experienced recurring nightmares about growing a beard and mustache. Soon it would be time for Jazz and her parents to make that decision about her taking puberty-blocking medication to end those bad dreams and worries.

One of the essential questions the endocrinologist or other clinician asks a young transitioning patient is, "Are you uncomfortable with the changes that are beginning to take place in your body?" By mid-2012, Jazz's response was a definite "Yes!"

So in June, when Jazz was nearing 12-years-old, the doctor performed a minor surgical procedure to place a subcutaneous (below the skin) implant into Jazz's left forearm.[95*] The tiny capsule would slowly release a special medication called *Supprelin*. This medicine blocks the brain from signaling the body's release of the male puberty chemical, the hormone *testosterone*. Suppressing this male hormone would prevent Jazz from beginning to develop like a man. The implanted capsule works for one to two years, during which time blood tests every few months determine if the correct level of medication is being maintained. (An alternative medicine, *Lupron*, is administered by injections given monthly or tri-monthly.)

Most patients do very well with the hormone blocker and usually experience no side effects. Other than blocking development of the body's male- (or female-) specific characteristics, children continue to grow in a normal fashion, although often not as much in height. First introduced in the Netherlands in the 1990s, and 2007 in the United States, this medication was originally used to treat children for another medical condition. Doctors report that the drug has an excellent safety record.

The purpose of blocking the onset of puberty is to give a child time to become older, more knowledgeable, and, it is thought, better able to make an informed decision about whether or not to continue the transition. (Some physicians describe this as "stopping the clock" or

---

*ABC's *20/20* cameras were present, filming for the "Listening to Jazz" documentary.

"pressing the pause button.") The blocker medication also provides the child and family more time to weigh the various options available to them, beyond just halting the puberty process.

Since the puberty blocker makes no permanent, irreversible changes, a child in transition could simply discontinue the suppressing medication, which would allow the body's natural puberty hormones to restart. Physicians believe it is important to keep this choice open in case the child changes their mind about transitioning.[13] This is known as *desisting.*

Does that often occur? As noted in Chapter 3 ("Gender Identity Disorder"), there are no reliable, conclusive, long-term research studies available to answer this and the many other questions about transgender and gender non-conforming youth. Only in the last few years have such investigations been initiated, and it will be some time, perhaps a decade, before the data becomes available to draw meaningful conclusions.

Without more definitive information, doctors and parents confront uncertainty when deciding on medical interventions for trans kids. Furthermore, it is not known if any side-effects may turn up many years later. As Jeanette Jennings has observed, this is all "uncharted territory," and it can be very difficult, even agonizing, for parents and physicians to make these medical decisions.

In the meantime, anecdotal reports from numerous children's healthcare providers indicate that it is actually quite rare for patients to have second thoughts about continuing on the puberty-suppressing medication. In fact, they say that most adolescents who use blockers end up going on to *cross-hormone therapy* (described in the following chapter).[72] According to Dr. Johanna Olson, the specialist who treats transgender youth, in her own years of practice she has only had one patient on hormone blockers decide to stop transitioning.[70]

The Jennings were advised to occasionally check with Jazz to see if she had any misgivings about taking the hormone blocker, and might want to continue on to male puberty. Her response to Jeanette was, "Mommy, why would I want to do *that*?" as if this were a crazy question to ask.[95] In July 2014, when the puberty blocker medication ran low, a new capsule was emplaced in Jazz's arm, and she was anticipating repeating this procedure when necessary in the years to come.[40.1]

Jazz's transition began at home around the age of three-and-a-half (probably the youngest as of that time). She has continued along the same path since then, including "social transition" at age five, going on the puberty blocker at age 11, and then replenishing the blocker medication implant. After more than 11 years of unwavering commitment to her transition, it was clear Jazz was not going to change her mind about continuing with this process.

Commenting on the hormone-suppressing medication, Jeanette said, "It's not a magic pill by any means." And as mentioned, the process of evaluating and judging the different medical interventions for Jazz is a difficult journey. "The whole hormone gamut is just uncharted territory. It's considered experimental. But it goes with the territory. I'd rather have to do something like that than experience the consequences of having her body develop like a man. I don't want her to look like that, and she doesn't want to look like that." [65]

Calling the drugs "extremely expensive," Jeanette stated that she was quoted $18,000 a year for the hormone-blockers in the subcutaneous form.[65] But the alternative shots are also quite costly. According to Jeanette, "At first insurance said no, and we're trying different avenues, we're trying to appeal." [65] The Jennings were eventually able to arrange insurance coverage for Jazz's medications.[50]

Another mom, Jennifer Kahler, went into greater detail about the typical expenses incurred by the transition process, most of which are often *not* covered by insurance.[72] The puberty blockers, depending on which medicine is used, cost thousands of dollars per year, as quoted to Jeanette. Families also commonly pick up the office fees of the pediatrician or other physician. Then there is the expense of cross-hormone treatment (discussed in the next chapter), and there can be costs for surgical procedures (also covered in another chapter). Receiving therapy from a gender specialist, a key element in transitioning, incurs an added cost per visit.

Another transition expense might be attorney's fees for resolving legal issues. These may involve such concerns as getting a name change and gender re-designation on the birth certificate and other official documents, as well as legal challenges that can arise both in school and later on in employment. Anyone who thinks being transgender is a "choice" has no idea of the obstacles and expense encountered by trans individuals.

Some transgender people have sought alternative, cost-saving sources for their medications, even purchasing illegal drugs off the street. That is an extremely dangerous prospect. Others have discovered there are suppliers located on the Internet, which can be a money-saving resource. However, going online to obtain blockers and cross-gender hormones (next chapter), and then taking these medications without medical supervision, is also a very risky approach, and is not recommended.

One excellent, safe alternative solution is for trans youth to seek medical services from one of the trans-health centers that have been established in major cities around the US and Canada. One of the first to open was Gender Management Services (GeMS) at Boston Children's Hospital, established by Dr. Norman Spack.[*] The advantage of these clinics is that they provide comprehensive services all under one roof, which is very convenient. Patients can be seen there by primary care doctors, pediatricians, endocrinologists, mental healthcare providers, and other necessary service providers such as legal advisors. There can also be a significant cost-savings when utilizing clinic services, compared to visiting individual doctors' offices.

---

[*] In 2007, Dr. Spack pioneered use of hormone blockers in the US, which he first learned about during a trip to the Netherlands in 2000.

The Blockers

Some endocrinologists have recently found other ways to reduce expenses for their patients' families. They are now prescribing *Vantas*, an alternative form of the very-costly puberty blocker *Supprelin*. Although Vantas is intended for adult males for another medical purpose, it is identical to Supprelin, and is available at a fraction of the cost. One parent reported applying to the Supprelin drug manufacturer for assistance, using a form provided by the doctor's office. She now obtains blockers at a substantial discount.

Just how effective is the puberty blocker for transgender kids like Jazz? For an example, there is a pair of identical twin boys named Jonas and Wyatt Maines, who are about three years older than Jazz. According to an article in *The Boston Globe*, Wyatt and Jazz share a lot in common. Wyatt began taking the blocker at 11-years-old, legally changed his name to Nicole (Nikki), and requested being called *she* instead of *he*.[13]

By age 14, the physical differences between Jonas and Nikki were dramatic, as reported in the *Globe*: "Jonas is handsome, Nicole pretty. Jonas is midway through puberty. His shoulders have broadened, his voice has deepened, and there's a shadow on his upper lip. He's 5 feet 6 with a size 11 shoe." Like Jazz, "Nicole is petite: 5 feet, 1 inch. She's got long, dark hair, and she wears girl's size 14-16." [13] A biography about Nikki, *Becoming Nicole*, by author and journalist Amy Ellis Nutt, was published in October 2015.

*****

Just as with Jazz's social transition, use of the puberty blocker brought Greg and Jeanette more criticism. But now that the Jennings were better-known in the media, the criticism came from both near and far. As with previous disapproval, this new wave of condemnation was from those who were intolerant and misinformed. In a recent televised discussion, the interviewer posed to Jazz's parents a commonly asked question: Isn't Jazz too young? Why not wait until she's an adult to make these life-altering decisions? [40.1]

Jeanette's reply was a sobering one. "Because Jazz might not be alive. She might not make it to adulthood. Going through male puberty would probably be the worst, most devastating thing that could happen to her." Jeanette added, "To have put Jazz through male puberty would be cruel, cruel." [40.1]

~Jazz Mergirl~

Chapter 17
Chemical Transition

Following administration of the hormone blockers, the next step in transition may be receiving *cross-gender hormones*, also known as *hormone-replacement therapy* (HRT). This process of *chemical transition* initiates the physical transition of a male body into a more feminine appearance (male-to-female, or MTF), such as Jazz desires. The opposite would apply for transitioning a female body to have more masculine features (female-to-male, or FTM). One news reporter explained, "It is the next big step – taking sex hormones of the opposite gender – that creates permanent changes that cannot be hormonally reversed." [13]

For this purpose, many doctors treating transgender patients follow the cautious protocol (the accepted methods) of the World Professional Association for Transgender Health (WPATH) *Standards of Care* (first published in 1979). The current edition of the handbook continues to recommend that this next phase of medical transitioning not occur until the individual is at least 16-years-old.[96] The logic behind this recommendation is that a patient that age will have the maturity and life experience to make wise and informed decisions, along with guidance from their parents and healthcare providers.

However, in accord with more recent medical findings and years of experience treating transgender youth, a number of pediatricians and other medical specialists have been rethinking this older protocol. They are now prescribing cross-gender hormones for adolescents as young as 12-years-old, which is closer to the age when puberty usually begins.[70]

The doctors' view is that, for some young patients like Jazz, withholding hormone therapy until age 16 would cause more psychological damage than doing any good. That is contrary to the physicians' oath to "do no harm." It's a matter of the child, their parents, the doctor, and possibly a gender therapist, determining if and when the time is right. It is a carefully-taken decision, and is based on the youth's level of maturity, mental health status, and individual needs. What is best for one patient may not be appropriate for another of the same age. "One-size-fits-all" policies are not useful.

During sixth grade at her new middle school, Jazz was going through what she later described as a most difficult, depressing emotional time.[50] That is a common experience for transgender adolescents. On the one hand, she was relieved that the hormone blockers prevented her from ever looking like a man. But her growth as a female appeared to be stuck on hold until age 16. At the same time that her girlfriends were entering puberty and starting to develop female characteristics, Jazz was feeling very depressed that she would have to wait a few more years for her own development to begin.

In her case, Jazz's doctors and her parents decided it would be best for her to start hormone-replacement therapy sooner, rather than waiting until she turned 16. This was a banner event that Jazz remembers to the day: Wednesday, March 6, 2013.[50] Jazz was 12 and one-half years old, around the time that normal female puberty is well underway.

In this subsequent stage of transition, a pediatrician or other physician *adds* to the blocker medication the female hormone called *estrogen*. The body normally releases this substance during a girl's puberty. Giving estrogen to a transgender patient causes various physical modifications to occur (similar to puberty), making a boy body begin to transform into a more girl-like appearance (MTF).[13] These physical alterations include breast development, and other changes in body shape, bones, muscles, and the texture of skin and hair, all of which become more feminine.

The opposite occurs if this involves a birth-assigned girl transitioning into a boy body (FTM). This requires receiving the male hormone *testosterone*, or "T," that causes development of male characteristics. In that situation, it is usually *not* necessary for a transitioning male to continue taking the very costly estrogen-suppressing blockers as part of their hormone treatment. Testosterone is such a powerful chemical that it generally offsets most naturally occurring female estrogen.[88]

Hormones are available in different formulations: injectable (shots), slow-release implants (under the skin), nasal sprays, pills, sublingual tablets (under the tongue), skin gels, and transdermal (skin) patches.[96] The most common and effective method of administering these transition drugs is by receiving hormone injections at home. The frequency and strength of these shots varies from patient to patient, some being prescribed with a twice-monthly injection, and others receiving a weekly dose. It's safest to administer testosterone as an injection because the pill form can stress the liver.

Sometimes physicians prescribe a combination of injections and pills. It can get fairly complicated, depending on the doctor's choice of medications, the patient's needs, and how their body responds to the drugs. In Jazz's situation, she began with just a daily low-dose estrogen pill, in addition to the medication provided by her puberty-blocking implant.[64.1] Her body has responded very well, with no significant side effects.[50] For the drugs to be effective, Jazz needs to take them for the rest of her life.[13]

Dr. Norman Spack, the Boston gender clinician, thinks very highly of the effect that cross-gender hormones bring about. "In my experience, patients just blossom physically and mentally when they get the hormones of the gender they affirm," Spack says. "It's quite amazing."[13]

Jazz told interviewers that while awaiting hormone therapy, she had been wearing a padded bra. She wanted to fit in better with other girls her age who were going through normal female puberty. Jazz was eagerly looking forward to experiencing those shape changes herself, which the hormones initiated. This worked out well for her. One year later, she was pleased that her much-sought-after development was underway, [43 / 50] although that padded bra still helps her self-image.

However, by the time Jazz was 14, she couldn't help noticing that most of her friends were physically maturing more quickly than she was. Under the best of circumstances, adolescent girls often feel insecure and competitive about their growth, but for Jazz, her chest size took on an even greater significance, and she grew impatient. She wanted her doctor to increase the strength of her daily estrogen pills.[40.1]

Then came time for her regular medical checkup in early 2015. Jazz gets her blood checked periodically to determine the level of the testosterone blocker, as well as the amount of testosterone and estrogen present. Her pediatric endocrinologist, Dr. Wil Charlton, shared the good news that there was no detectable amount of the male hormone testosterone. Jazz and her parents were relieved to hear that news. [40.1]

But the doctor found Jazz's female estrogen level was below normal. He explained this is actually a good sign. Too much estrogen given to a young person causes the *growth plates* at the ends of their long bones to close prematurely, halting any more gain in height. Jazz was only about 5 foot, 2 inches tall. If she would be patient, her natural growth in height would be maximized, and then later on, an increase in estrogen would promote more of the breast development she desired. Although disappointed, Jazz knew it was best to continue with the low-dose hormone pills to allow some additional height gain.[40.1]

By mid-2015, when the Jennings returned to see Dr. Charlton, Jazz measured 5 foot, 3½ inches, which he estimated was about her maximum height. Jazz now had a choice to make. She could remain on the low-dose estrogen, in hopes of gaining a bit more height, or switch to a stronger daily hormone pill and initiate more rapid breast development. Jazz decided on those "bigger boobs" she kept talking about. The doctor agreed, but warned that more estrogen frequently results in patients experiencing mood swings.[40.1]

Toward the end of the appointment, Dr. Charlton addressed one other concern Jazz has often expressed. She was worried that her testosterone blocker would somehow fail, causing a sudden surge in the male hormone, and rapid growth of coarse hair on her body. The doctor reassured his young patient that he would continue carefully monitoring both her "T" levels and the hormone suppressant, and would spot any fluctuations *well-before* a change in appearance could occur.[40.1]

*****

The WPATH *Standards of Care* requires trans patients satisfy several eligibility and readiness criteria (rules) to qualify for hormone therapy. Before a patient can begin taking the medication, a mental healthcare professional (counselor, therapist, or psychologist) must write a letter of recommendation to the physician who will be providing the medical treatment.[90] Besides obtaining this letter, a patient needs to:

1. Be at least 16 years of age. (As previously noted, a number of doctors are now prescribing hormones for patients as young as 12.)

2. Understand what hormones can and cannot do medically, and understand their social benefits and risks.

3. Participate in a minimum of three months of psychotherapy (counseling).

4. An acceptable alternative to such counseling is a documented, three-month, "24/7," real-life experience expressing the gender with which the person identifies.

5. Show stable or improved mental health.

6. Demonstrate the ability to take prescribed hormones in a responsible manner.[90]

After a patient meets these criteria and undergoes a basic physical examination, a physician will then prescribe the medication. Parents often ask if there are possible physical side effects from administering these cross-gender hormones (whether estrogen for MTF or testosterone for FTM). According to trans-youth medical specialist Dr. Johanna Olson:

> Certainly, we talk about risks with patients, but in cases like this, it's really important to know that actually these medications are relatively safe, especially when you compare them to the lifetime that people will have if they don't do a hormonal transition.[73]

Dr. Maddie Deutsch from the UC San Francisco Center of Excellence for Transgender Health, points out that many trans youth have been on numerous antidepressants and other medications for years. For those kids, resolving the gender dysphoria with blockers and cross-hormone treatment is actually much more successful and has far fewer side effects than taking all those other drugs, or denying any treatment at all.[63]

When Jazz was seven and the topic of side effects came up, Jeanette had to explain to her daughter that, if she went on this path of chemical transition, the treatment would leave her infertile. That would mean Jazz could not make her own baby. This realization makes both her and Jeanette very sad,[68/95] but it's an unavoidable outcome of taking these hormones. (The same infertility occurs to FTM transgender patients receiving testosterone.)

Some years later, in a Twitter live chat, Jazz tweeted: "As much as I embrace my uniqueness and love myself, the hardest part about being transgender is not being able to have my own biological child."[52] Later Jazz was asked by a journalist from *Cosmopolitan* magazine, "Why does not being able to have your own biological child stand out now, even though you're so young?"[81]

> It's really hard for me to look at that because with such an amazing mom, I always wanted to be the greatest mom ever. People say, 'Oh, you can always adopt,' and I completely agree with that. I can adopt. But, like, I'll

never have that moment where she comes out of me, and I can say, 'That's my baby.' But since my sister has my same DNA (genes), I'm convincing her to carry the baby for me.[81] (In fact, Ari now says she would be willing to do that for Jazz. She's an amazing big sister.) [40.1]

However this all turns out for Jazz, that's a decision to be made many years from now. "I want to be the mother of my own child. I know if I adopt, I will still be a great mother anyways, and I'll give them all the love I have inside." [76]

Regarding having to tell her little girl about infertility, Jeanette rhetorically asked, "Why should a seven-year-old have to know that? Being transgender is *really* difficult, and I don't think people understand all it is. We look happy, but there's been a lot of pain and decisions to make." [68] * On a *Huff Post* webcast, Jeanette added, "Jazz is the bravest, most courageous person I've met in my life." [63]

---

*Caitlyn Jenner was quoted in a June 2015 *Vanity Fair* article saying, "I wish I were kind of normal. It would be so much simpler."

~Jazz Mergirl~

Chapter 18

Gender-Affirming Surgery

What pathway might Jazz take beyond her chemical (hormone) transition? Some transgender individuals are pleased with the body image that results from hormone treatment alone. Some even decide against a chemical transition at all, being satisfied with their social transition. Others will never be comfortable without additional changes to bring their physical appearance more completely into conformity with their gender identity. It has been reported that about one-third of those in the transgender community take this next step,[24] although more would probably do so if they could afford these procedures.

This sort of alteration, which goes beyond social and chemical transition, requires reconstructive surgery. Depending on the amount of reconstruction that is needed, such a surgical transition may involve more than one operation. However, using blockers to halt, or avoid puberty altogether, can significantly reduce the extent of surgery that is necessary. This can also lessen the cost of these modifications, which amounts to thousands of dollars per procedure.

Having had her puberty suppressed, Jazz will need less of these surgical alterations, should she decide to go that route. This is one of the major advantages Jazz and many others of her generation will have, as compared to older transgender people whose puberty was *not* stopped.

The current, widely-accepted WPATH protocol (medical policy) is to wait until the patient is at least 18-years-old. That is the "adult age of consent" that doctors have been requiring for people to make such a life-altering decision to undergo reconstructive operations. As of this time, when insurance companies *do* cover these procedures (which is not common), it is only for those of consenting age.

Waiting until age 18 has its advantages. If the patient has been taking hormones since 16 or younger, then by age 18, the cross-gender drugs will have brought about much of the physical transition that is expected from these medications. That way, the medical team and patient will have a better idea about what surgical modifications are still required to achieve the desired appearance.

Then again, German pop star Kim Petras is noteworthy for having been permitted to undergo such surgery in 2008, at age 16, the youngest person to do so at the time. And now in the US, the *New York Times* reports, "Several doctors said they had performed surgery on minors." One specialist, Dr. Christine McGinn of Pennsylvania, estimated that she has carried out more than 30 operations on patients under 18, split equally between MTFs and FTMs.[26] This re-evaluation of WPATH age guidelines for surgery is in keeping with the decision by some doctors to prescribe cross-gender hormones for youth well-below the recommended age of 16.

The primary purpose of such an operation is to "reduce the discrepancy between an individual's physical body and gender identity."[96] For many trans patients, the most significant alteration they opt for is reshaping their genitals. This entails a complicated, four-hour operation that is called *sex* or *gender reassignment surgery* (SRS / GRS). The newer, preferred terms are *gender-affirming surgery* and *gender-confirmation surgery* (GCS). These surgical methods were first attempted in Europe as long ago as the 1930s, but were only approved by the American Medical Association in 1972. Many technical advances have taken place since that time, but there is still much improvement to be made, especially for FTMs.

For Jazz, one side benefit of an operation like this is that her body would no longer be able to produce testosterone, the male hormone. Therefore, she would be able to discontinue relying on the very costly testosterone blocker implants, and just take estrogen.[64.1] Although the effects of taking hormone blockers long-term are still being researched, there is some concern about damage that may occur after years of use. Being able to surgically stop testosterone production, instead of continuing on the blockers, would likely be the safer option.

Will Jazz decide to take this next step in the transition process? She has long-expressed significant dysphoria (discomfort) with "what's between her legs." As mentioned in a previous chapter, even as young as two-years-old, Jazz had asked Mom, "When is the Good Fairy going to change my penis into a vagina?" [94] So there is a good chance that Jazz will eventually opt for some form of gender-affirmation surgery. Yet, in recent interviews and on a visit with her doctor, she shared some uncertainty about making this life-changing choice.[40.1 / 64.1] Jazz knows she needs time to give this a lot more thought. Her parents say they will support whatever decision she makes about pursuing such modifications.

Another surgical procedure might be needed to enhance breast shape and size, if desired. For MTFs like Jazz, male hormones released at birth may limit just how much breast tissue can grow in response to the administration of female estrogen hormones.[96] As a consequence, Jazz might not be pleased with the amount of natural growth that is triggered by hormone treatment alone. She should have a much better idea about this situation by the age of 16 or 17, four or more years after starting cross-hormone therapy.

On the other hand, female-to-male (FTM) patients often elect to have a breast *reduction* operation to create a more masculine physique. Breast surgery is commonly referred to as "top surgery," and the other type is called "bottom surgery."

The WPATH *Standards of Care* highly recommends that surgical procedures go hand-in-hand with psychological counseling (which Jazz has received over the years of her transition). This is because "research has found that if individuals bypass psychotherapy in their gender dysphoria treatment, they often feel lost and confused when their surgical treatments are complete." [96] For many transgender individuals, the ideal combination of interventions for gender dysphoria is counseling, hormones, and surgery, and "the overall level of satisfaction is very high." [96]

One interesting facet of gender-confirmation surgery is that in some states, like where Jazz was born, current, outmoded law requires a person undergo this procedure *before* they can legally change the sex recorded on their birth certificate. Should Jazz undergo GCS, she can then apply for a new, corrected birth certificate. Then again, federal regulations were updated in 2010 to permit a more reasonable, enlightened approach to designating sex on official documents. That is why Jazz's US passport already lists her as *female*, no surgery required.[95]

While on this topic, one more issue to discuss is the public's fascination with what a transgender person has "between their legs." One fact that was most notable when doing research for this book was seeing just how widespread and keen is this interest. Jazz and most other trans individuals would like cisgender (non-transgender) people to understand their point of view: It's what's between their ears, not what's in their pants, which defines them or makes them who they truly are. It matters far more how a person thinks and identifies within their mind, rather than what body parts they have. This concept is the opposite of long-held cultural norms, which are slowly evolving to become more accepting of transgender and gender-expansive individuals.

Transgender people often say that it gets very tiring to have these same inquiries about their anatomy repeated over and over. And those posing such questions can be insensitive, intrusive, and rude. But Jazz has been remarkably patient and forthright in her responses and attitude, determined to spread her message of understanding and acceptance. She is an amazing, brave person.

That being said, let's put all those prying questions to rest. Here are the basic answers, put in as delicate and respectful a manner as possible. While this is about Jazz Jennings, it applies to many, but by no means all, MTF transgender people. As of this writing, Jazz has *not* had any sort of gender-affirming surgery. As previously mentioned, she's still too young, and needs more time to make such decisions. So yes, she does still have the male private parts, or, as Jazz sometimes says, "The. P. Word." [87] However, the testosterone blockers given to Jazz continue to prevent development of male characteristics, and the estrogen hormones she takes keep enhancing the feminine appearance she desires.

Since Jazz identifies as female, she uses the women's restroom facilities, in the privacy of a locked stall, and uses those facilities just like any other female would. [50]

Again, identifying as a girl, Jazz wears girl clothes, and that includes what's underneath. When changing clothes at school for gym and sports activities, as noted before, she also uses a locked stall in the girl's bathroom adjacent to the girl's locker room. [50] This is for her safety and privacy, and to prevent any sort of discomfort on the part of other students. Perhaps the day will come when that too is not such an issue.

When swimming in a pool or at the beach, Jazz always puts on swim shorts or a skirt. However, hormone treatment has given her an upper body she is pleased can now be covered by the top part of a girl's swimsuit, although she often wears a cover-up.[40.1]

~Jazz Mergirl~

Chapter 19
Filmed Appearances, 2012 – 2013

Over time, the more Jazz participated in media-related activities, the more comfortable and confident she became appearing there. She also learned from her mom about the power that media can have, and saw the potential of social media for sharing her story and spreading her message. That's when Jazz decided to make her own YouTube video, with help from Jeanette. Titled *Message to Obama*, the three-minute video was uploaded onto Jeanette's channel on May 24, 2012.[*] The YouTube summary reads:

> This is a video message from Jazz, an 11-year-old transgender girl. She talks about her life experiences and the challenges she's met through the discrimination she has faced. Jazz is a brave little girl with a very big message. This video was sent to the White House to educate our government and President Obama about transgender children.[36.1]

The introductory words to Mr. Obama were: "Hi, I am Jazz. I am 11-years-old. I was born a boy, but I live as a girl," and she proceeded

---

[*] The inspirational theme song used was "Carry On" by the group Fun.

to tell her story about being transgender.[*] Just as with the first 2008 YouTube video Jeanette made of seven-year-old Jazz, this one generated both appreciative, supportive responses, and also those that were religion-based criticisms, or were hate-filled comments.

When later asked about this, Jazz observed, "Yeah, on the YouTube video comments section, some people who are less understanding actually say very nasty and rude comments. It definitely hurts to hear them say that they would want to kill me or something like that." [95] Jeanette added, "They can't wrap their mind around the idea of a transgender kid. And I want to tell everybody they are wrong and show them Jazz, because when people meet her, they start to get it." [95]

After Jazz got older, wiser, and more "thick-skinned," she came up with a spin on this hate speech. Now her response is along the lines of, "The haters are my motivators." Turning a negative into a positive, Jazz observed, "We need the hate so we know how much work there is to do and to encourage us to keep creating change."[50] Jazz was recently asked by an online magazine reporter, "How do you deal with haters on YouTube and Twitter?" She replied:

> A lot of people say, 'Jazz, you should delete the haters'
> comments because they are venomous to your page.'

---

[*] Three years later, in his State of the Union address, Mr. Obama became the first president ever to make an official reference using the term *transgender* and to speak about ensuring LGBT rights. On June 24, 2015, Jazz attended a Pride-Month reception at the White House, and her comments were edited into a video posted on the WH website.

When I see someone that is just completely intolerable
or is cursing me off, there's nothing I can do, so I either
ignore it or deal with it. But I never delete it.[81]

Applying this same philosophy, Jazz gives this advice to others
suffering hatred and discrimination: "It is very difficult, but you just
have to stay positive and get past what they say. Don't let it affect you.
Find friends who will love and accept you." [50]

Eventually, Jazz set up her own YouTube channel (Jazz Jennings).
This is a visual art form that she has worked to master, and she has
become proficient using iMovie Maker software and other apps. Jazz
went on to create several new videos, often with help from her pal Kaci,
whom she has known since preschool. Jazz's social media following
continues to grow as she becomes more prominent on television and
online. As of this writing, her YouTube channel had over 150,000
subscribers, more than four times the amount from just three months
before.

These YouTube videos can be grouped into four genres. The first
type is those that have a serious purpose, such as *Message to Obama*,
Letter to the World, the *Q&A* video, a number of Jazz's speeches, and
her numerous television appearances. These will be further addressed in
a later chapter. The next genre is the do-it-yourself (DIY) arts-and-crafts
instructional videos, which will also be covered in a subsequent chapter.
Kaci was instrumental in helping Jazz film the third kind of videos,

which are mermaid-tail underwater segments.[*] One of these uploads had 1.5 million views as of the latest count. And the last genre consists of entertaining, humorous shorts, such as a *Bloopers* episode that she recorded. Jazz has quite a quirky sense of humor. She can be really funny.

But Jazz can be very compassionate as well. In her *Q&A* YouTube, one of the questions she responded to was from a female-to-male (FTM) adolescent going through unwanted puberty without family acceptance or support. Jazz suggested kids in this situation find another person, maybe an adult, a friend, or peer, to provide that backing. She acknowledged never having had that problem with her own family, but empathized that this lack of support at such a challenging time must be very, very difficult to deal with. Her eyes glistening with tears, she said:

> I feel awful. I can't even imagine going through puberty
> of the opposite sex. I'm here for you. I'm fighting for
> you, you know. That's what I do every day. I just hope
> you can feel safe and happy, and I hope you can feel the
> love of society.[42]

In mid-2012, about eight months after filming *I Am Jazz* for OWN, the Jennings family once again agreed to an interview with ABC's Barbara Walters. Having already done the 2007 "My Secret Self" documentary, they were comfortable agreeing to participate in this

---

[*]Jazz was inspired to film these by having previously done the beautiful underwater sequence for the *I Am Jazz* OWN documentary.

second *20/20* program. Titled "Transgender at 11: Listening to Jazz," the 13-minute segment briefly reviewed tape of the original show from when Jazz was just six-years-old. Back then, she was a quiet, shy, and reserved kindergartner, at the beginning of her transition. By the time of "Listening to Jazz," viewers saw a totally different, 11-year-old fifth grader. Jeanette proudly described her this way: "Vibrant, happy, full of life, self-confident, beautiful, glowing, so feminine." [95]

The sit-down interview with Barbara Walters was planned to coincide with the Jennings' trip to New York in June 2012. Jazz was scheduled to receive a prestigious award and appear in the annual New York Gay Pride Parade, so the Jennings family was able to meet with Barbara at ABC's Manhattan studios. It was a very exciting experience. Additional filmed sequences were shot in the Jennings' home, in two doctors' offices, at school, and on the soccer field. Barbara's narration was later edited in to these scenes.[95]

The "Transgender at 11" documentary explored several important concerns that faced this tween-age girl: How was her transition going, did she experience any discrimination in the process, what was involved in beginning to receive medical interventions, was she now allowed to play girl's soccer and use the girl's restroom at school, and were there concerns about dating boys?[95] These topics are all addressed elsewhere in this book.

Although ABC originally planned to air "Listening to Jazz" in September 2012, it was delayed two times because of scheduling problems, including a hurricane hitting New York. The *20/20* special was finally broadcast in mid-January 2013. The documentary earned a GLAAD Media Award that year, just like "My Secret Self" had done six years earlier.

Jeanette and Jazz's 2011 appearance on the *Dr. Drew on Call* program was the first time they had participated in a broadcast panel discussion. About a year later, in April 2013, they took part in another on-air panel conversation, this time a videophone webcast sponsored by *Huff Post Live*. There were five participants in the discussion, moderated by the Huffington Post reporter, Alicia Mendez. In addition to Jazz and Jeanette were: Kim Pearson, who is the parent of a transgender child and a consultant on trans issues, Dr. Anne Dohrenwend, clinical psychologist and author, and Dr. Maddie Deutsch, Clinical Lead at the UC San Francisco Center of Excellence for Transgender Health.[63]

What followed was a very interesting, hour-long discussion among the panelists and Alicia Mendez. She was well-prepared and informed, and asked lots of discerning and thought-provoking questions, but always in a sensitive and empathetic manner. To give viewers background information and context, Alicia began by interviewing Jazz and then Jeanette. This segment was interspersed with film clips from the ABC and OWN documentaries.[63]

Recognizing that there is a great deal of ignorance and misunderstanding within the public sphere, Alicia then asked the experts to weigh in. Dr. Deutsch explained that years of research and anecdotal evidence indicate being transgender is *not* a choice, and that denying children the opportunity to be their authentic selves only brings about pain, suffering, and self-harm. The doctor went on to discuss how gender dysphoria is diagnosed, and what medical interventions are available.[63]

Dr. Deutsch agrees with Jeanette that parents need to be their child's first and best advocate, and to stand up to the bullying that often occurs. But it is also common for parents to need time to process their child's transition. Like Jeanette, both Dr. Deutsch and Dr. Dohrenwend see attitudes changing for the better over the last few years, first toward the LGB community, and more recently, toward transgender people.

In May 2013, about a month after the *Huff Post* webcast, Jazz and Jeanette took part in another videophone discussion, this time on a *Transition Radio-TV* webcast. The interview was unique for the Jennings because the two journalists who hosted this conversation, Mark Angelo and Jessica Lynn Cummings, are also transgender. They call their program, "The show for trans folks, by trans folks." When talking with Jazz, their own trans experience gave them a totally different perspective, asking insightful questions and sharing their own stories as only other transgender individuals could.[1] A number of Jazz and Jeanette's replies have been included in other portions of this book.

Both Mark and Jessica indicated that they did not have the acceptance and love of their families when they were transitioning. That revelation led to a discussion about the dramatic contrast between those kids who are rejected by their parents, and those like Jazz who receive unconditional love and support.[1] That has been shown to make a huge difference in the mental health of transgender youth.

When Mark, referring to Jazz, asked Jeanette about "being given this wonderful gift," Jazz got a mischievous look on her face, and muttered, "I'm in a box … (long pause) … with a bow." Everyone laughed at that. But the conversation concluded on a much more serious note. Jazz and Jeanette reiterated their message for parents to be accepting and loving of their children, and to allow those kids to lead the way as they unfold their own individual gender identities.[1]

And Jazz once again advised gender-nonconforming youth to be accepting and loving of themselves. If their parents are not supportive, then she encourages young people to seek help from extended family, friends, teachers, school counselors, or others who can give assistance, or to call one of the nation-wide trans suicide hotlines for guidance.[1] (See "Resources" section.)

The Jennings Family, July 2014.
Below clockwise: Jazz, Greg, Ari, Griffen, Jeanette, Sander.

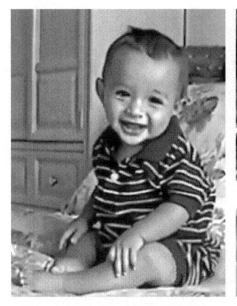 

Above: 2001, 5 months old. **Below**: 2001, 16 months, w/Ari's dress-up shoes & unsnapped onesie.	**Above**: 2004, about 3½ years old. **Below**: 2004, about 3 years.

 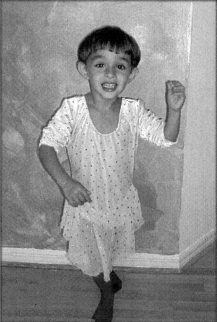

Above: Jazz's coming-out 5th birthday party, Oct. 16, 2005.

Above: Preschool Dad's Night, Disney's 'Belle,' 2006, age 5½.
Above Right: Jazz's 1st "outside" dress, 2006, age 5½.

Above: Tutu dress, age almost 6 years old.

Above & Below: "My Secret Self," ABC *20/20* interview with Barbara Walters, April 27, 2007, age 6½.

Above: Kindergarten, 2006, age 6 years old.

Top: Cheerleader, kinder, 2007, age 6.
Right: Benched from soccer, 2008-2010.
Below: Reinstated, 2011.

Above: Rosie O'Donnell Show, with Chaz Bono (left), Jazz, Jeanette, and Rosie, November 2011, age 11.

Below: Colin Higgins Youth Courage Award @ Trevor w/ Thomas Roberts and Anthony Rapp, June 2012, age 11½.

"Listening to Jazz," ABC *20/20* interview with Barbara Walters, January 2013, age 11½.

Above Left: GLAAD Media Awards, April 2013, age 12½.
Above Right: GLAAD Awards, with Jennifer Lawrence.

Below: Pres. Clinton (with Chelsea) requested meeting Jazz,
GLAAD Media Awards, April 2013, age 12½.

Below: Logo TV Trailblazer Youth Award, w/Laverne Cox, June 27, 2014, age 13½.

Above: Jazz Mergirl, August 2013, almost 13.
Below: July 2014, almost 14.

by Michael Price

Above: *I Am Jazz*, Books & Books signing, September 7, 2014.
Below: Reading *I Am Jazz*, Katie Couric interview, Oct. 2014.

Above: Jazz Mergirl, August 2014.

Below: Interview with Katie Couric, Oct. 17, 2014, age 14.

Below: Premier of *I Am Jazz*, July 2015, w / author.

Jazz is an amazing, self-taught artist. She has become an
accomplished portraitist in just a few years' time.

by Jazz, 2012

by Jazz, 2012

Work in progress, by Jazz 2014

Chapter 20

Filmed Appearances, 2014 – 2015

A year or so went by before the Jennings agreed to participate in another televised interview, this one to be shown in Scandinavia. In March 2014, Renée Nyberg, an acclaimed Swedish television journalist, visited with Jazz and her family for a discussion that was later broadcast on Sweden's TV3 channel.[68] Renée has a quiet, intimate style of interviewing that made this particular documentary one that was especially personal and very touching. It's unfortunate the video is no longer available for viewing from TV3, although Jazz included a brief segment in her YouTube *Story of Jazz – A Transgender Child*.

Toward the end of Renée Nyberg's interview, she asked Jazz, "If I were to have a genie in a bottle, and you were granted three wishes, what would you wish for?" Jazz's remarkable response, in Renée's words, "just blew me away." Jazz said:

> I would *not* wish to *not* be transgender, 'cause I like the way I am. It's the person I am. And I'm proud of myself and what I've accomplished. It's made me a braver person, being transgender. And it's just become a part of me.[68]

As this exchange demonstrates, whenever Jazz is interviewed, she replies in a confident, forthright manner. As one magazine reporter observed, "She has the composure of girls twice her age. During interviews on the subject of being transgender, she doesn't stumble over her words, won't back down from tough questions, and speaks with authority and even wisdom." [84]

Around the same time as the Swedish TV interview, there was a pre-publication listing on Amazon.com for the forthcoming children's picture book, *I Am Jazz*, co-authored by Jessica Herthel and Jazz Jennings. A number of different media events and interviews were arranged to publicize the book's September 2014 release. For the next few months, all those book-related activities kept Jazz and Jeanette even busier than usual. More details about these events are covered in the chapter "I Am Jazz – The Book."

After all of the book promotions had quieted down a bit, TLC cable (The Learning Channel) released a press statement on March 12, 2015, announcing a new television program, initially titled *All That Jazz*, but later renamed *I Am Jazz*. This 11-episode summer-season docuseries would star Jazz, and feature the entire Jennings family, and Jazz's maternal grandparents.

Years ago, when first told that their grandchild was transgender, Grandpa Jack and Grandma Jacky had difficulty understanding and accepting this revelation. But they came to embrace Jazz's transition, and have been totally supportive ever since.[22] In fact, when being interviewed during filming, Grandpa Jack became emotional in expressing his opinion that the Jennings were right to share their story with the public. "Why is this right?" he was asked. "Because Jazz is special." [40.1]

How did this TV series come about? Jeanette explained to an ezine reporter that she and Greg had long-considered doing something new for television because of Jazz's determination and enthusiasm to share her story and message [8.1] She was already a talented personality with a growing presence on social media, especially her popular YouTube channel.

Another motivation for doing a television show was that at the time, there just wasn't anything like *I Am Jazz* on TV that could go more in depth about being transgender. Greg and Jeanette knew if anyone could succeed with this, it would be their daughter. [8.1] So when TLC producers approached the Jennings in late 2014, the family was already receptive to the idea of doing a TV series. Jazz had just turned 14, and she was ready for this new challenge. [8.1]

At the same time, Jazz later acknowledged, "That was a very, very hard decision because this would completely obliterate whatever normal life we had before." [40.1] But agreeing to do the television program would be worth it. "We wanted to share the story, which is the message of love and tolerance and respecting transgender individuals for the people they are." [40.1]

Preliminary filming for the groundbreaking *I Am Jazz* TV series began soon after an agreement was signed, and there was even a film crew at the Jennings' home in March 2015, during spring break, when Jeanette and Jazz were away in New York. They were being interviewed by Thomas Roberts on the online streaming network Shift, on a program called *Out There*. The Jennings also made an appearance with Nancy Redd on a *Huff Post Live* webcast. These interviews, and a March 26th appearance in Los Angeles on Meredith Vieira's television talk show, were arranged to promote the upcoming TLC cable program.

Thomas Roberts chatted one-on-one with Jazz for 12 minutes, and then Jeanette joined them for the second 12-minute segment. Of course they talked about all of the media-related happenings going on in Jazz's life, and what it's like for her as a trans student and teenager.[77.1]

One first-time topic Thomas broached was inquiring about Jazz's relationship with her older sister and twin brothers. Because of their many accomplishments in school and sports, Jazz feels that a high level of expectations to keep up with them has landed on her shoulders. While her siblings are all very supportive and protective of Jazz, she did admit to having a lot of squabbles over the years with her brother, Sander. But she knows he loves her, and she is very proud of him, Griffen, and Ari.[77.1]

Another question Thomas posed led to a discussion about the public's fascination with transgender anatomy. As previously mentioned, Jazz shares the same feeling as many other transgender folks that they would just as soon the public not be so focused on body parts. They are called "private parts" for a reason. Once again, Jazz made the case that what's in a person's mind and heart, not their pants, is what makes them who they are.[77.1] In another interview, Jazz added, "Gender is so much bigger than that. It's like, 'Don't judge a book by their cover, and don't judge a person by their genitals.' " [81]

Talking with Nancy Redd on the March 2015 *Huff Post Live* webcast, Jazz explained her family's hopes for what the new TV series *I Am Jazz* would accomplish. "What we want to portray is that we are just a normal family," but at the same time, "Being transgender is unique, and it's okay to express who you are. I hope the show can make a difference for kids who *are* struggling, no matter what their differences are." [76] Jeanette added her aspirations for the show's outcome:

> Those families that are questioning and don't understand, we hope that they can see us and say, 'You know what? They (the Jennings) can do this. I can too, and I'm just going to try my best to accept my child the way they accepted Jazz.' We want happy endings. We don't want any more suicides, murders, death. So that's why we're doing this TV series.[76]

A few weeks before the docuseries was to air, Jeanette elaborated about the Jennings' momentous decision to participate in this groundbreaking program. In a newspaper interview, she said:

We put ourselves out there. We've done it. We've taken the leap of faith. I feel it's the right thing to do. If exposing our lives to the public can save lives, then we're all for it.[80]

TLC's docuseries *I Am Jazz* debuted on Wednesday, July 15, 2015. This first episode was a one-hour special that introduced viewers to Jazz and the Jennings family. Subsequent weekly shows consisted of two back-to-back, half-hour episodes, and then there were two, one-hour installments at the end.[40.1] Some of the family's remarks are included in this chapter and elsewhere in the book.

Topics incorporated into the series included the ordinary difficulties Jazz faced as a teen about to enter high school, such as going through puberty, body image, and concerns about boys and dating. In addition, the docuseries explored the added, not-so-ordinary challenges Jazz and her family confront because she is transgender. For example, a film crew accompanied the Jennings on visits to the pediatric endocrinologist, and cameras were even present when Jazz met with her gender therapist, Dr. Volker.[40.1] As Jeanette stated, the family really did give up privacy in order to educate the public and save lives.

Jazz brought the season to a close on the 10th-episode finale, with a big pool party celebrating middle-school graduation and the beginning of high school. She ended on an upbeat note, saying:

You know what? I'm ready for high school. Sometimes you're going to have bad moments, and sometimes great moments. But with my friends and the support of everyone that I have, *I've got this.* I'm gonna be cool.[40.1]

There was one more *I Am Jazz* episode to complete the summer season. This one-hour program, titled "The Family Tells All," was a compilation of several interview sessions with Greg and Jeanette, Jazz, her sister Ari and the twins, and then Jazz's grandparents. Kate Snow, the TLC correspondent, was very likeable and warm, and posed incisive, thought-provoking questions. The Q&A special focused on four subjects: Jazz's early struggles in her transition, her role as an activist for the young transgender community, how the family responds to the critics, and what lies ahead for Jazz, including the medical decisions she will need to make.[40.1]

As the TLC summer docuseries came to a close, Jazz had the final say. She was once again articulate and passionate about her cause:

> Right now we're at the forefront of the civil rights movement when it comes to transgender individuals. I feel like people are finally starting to change their perspective in the sense that they're becoming accepting and loving of people for who they are. It's great to see that change.
>
> I hope in the future when I have kids, I could say, you know there was a time where I couldn't live my life as

myself, but now I can just be me, and I want them to know that.[40.1]

I Am Jazz was enthusiastically received by its audience (1.5 million viewers for the premier, and an average of almost 1 million for the following installments). The series was well-regarded by TV reviewers. In the entertainment publication *Variety*, critic Brian Lowry gave the series a "thumbs up," calling it a "sensitively constructed series. Simply told and heartfelt."[59.1] *TIME* magazine's entertainment reviewer James Poniewozik wrote, "*I Am Jazz* is an engaging story of a teen girl who has transitioned." Poniewozik observed that the show chooses "to teach to the curious rather than preach to the converted," and so, "It is also the story of everyone else, transitioning."[74.1] Will there be a Season Two of *I Am Jazz*? At the time of this writing, no indication had been given by TLC about further commitments.

The same week the TLC *I Am Jazz* docuseries was announced, another major media development involving Jazz Jennings took place. Both Jazz and the advertising agency for Johnson & Johnson's "Clean and Clear" released press statements that she would be featured in that product's ongoing "See the Real Me" social media campaign. This skincare line is marketed to girls and young women, ages 12–24.[66] On *Out There*, Jeanette shared with Thomas Roberts that the ad agency had reached out to Jazz, and "interviewed her a couple of times" prior to offering a role.[77.1]

Before her participation was revealed, Jazz had already filmed two powerful and upbeat, one-minute spots that play on YouTube and via Facebook. One of them ends with the tagline, "I'm Jazz. See the real me." This video series aims to build confidence in the target age group by encouraging girls to "be comfortable in their own skin." That is something quite apropos for Jazz to speak about. For authenticity sake, only non-actors were used in these short documentaries, and they all have an exceptional story to tell.[66] Jazz has proven to be a perfect spokesperson for this ad campaign.

Jazz's appearance on NBC's *Meredith Vieira Show* on March 26 was a six-minute, emotion-packed segment that began with a brief video summary of her life so far. In Meredith's words, Jazz is "a trailblazer who wants everyone to be brave enough to be themselves." [92]

When introduced by Meredith, Jazz received an enthusiastic standing ovation from the audience, easing some of her admitted nervousness. Both Jazz and Meredith were obviously taken aback and moved by this spontaneous show of love. "People are so proud of you for being who you are, and for helping other people." [92]

Among the questions Meredith posed was asking Jazz how she is treated by other students at school. While "most are accepting," Jazz shared that it's not unusual for her to be subjected to rude remarks or to be excluded, especially by some boys. They might hug her friends, but at best, just give Jazz a "high five." That kind of rejection really hurts. But Jazz's reaction to that is: "I just have to keep moving forward and not care what they think. If I stay strong, and be myself, then their opinion doesn't matter at all. And that's what I do everyday." [92] Of course, that's easier said than done.

Replying to Meredith's inquiry about youth reaching out to her for help, Jazz's moving response was:

> A lot of times I get messages from kids who are struggling. Sometimes they say they walk in front of a street full of cars, or they're about to jump out of a window, and they say the reason they didn't do it was because of Jazz. That's why I keep sharing my stories, because I know I'm making a difference and creating change and helping those kids. I tell them to stay strong and love themselves, because no matter what, if they stay positive, things *will* get better.[92]

Asked by Meredith how she reacts to critics who have said she was too young to know anything about her gender identity, Jazz forcefully declared, "What I say to that is, *they* don't define me. *I* define myself. I know what's going on inside, not them." [92]

Meredith Vieira observed that Jazz is one very confident person, and then segued into discussing the "Clean and Clear" project. "I know you are hoping to reach a lot more people with this 'See the Real Me' campaign. What has it meant on a personal level to be asked to be part of this?" Jazz answered, "Well, the 'See the Real Me' campaign is about girls finding the courage to be their true selves. I was able to find myself and be who I was." [92]

In a *Huffington Post* article about being featured in the "Clean and Clear" video, Jazz stated:

> I feel really honored to be part of the 'See the Real Me' campaign. It's really amazing, as it helps many teen girls who are struggling. It helps them to find themselves and be true to who they are. I hope they can learn to be brave and not care what other people think about them, because if they just stay positive and spread love, then others will be true friends who will accept them no matter what. [67]

Having participated in so many documentaries and interviews raises the question about what it's like for members of the media to work with Jazz and her family. Michael Price, a photographer commissioned for a photo shoot of the Jennings family, commented about this:

> Working as a professional photographer for the past 30 years, I thought I had been exposed to all facets of the human condition. Meeting Jazz was truly an unexpected and unique experience. What I found was a truly supportive and loving family, parents and siblings very comfortable with Jazz's identity and journey. Jazz was a delight to work with throughout the photographic process. [75]

~Jazz Mergirl~

Chapter 21

The Art of Jazz

Jeanette Jennings has often expressed her opinion that transgender kids are unusually bright, talented, and creative people. Jazz is certainly an example of that. Her social media contain numerous photos of Jazz's artistry and engaging YouTube videos.

In the past, Jazz enjoyed singing and dancing in school groups, but no longer has the time or interest to pursue those activities. She does have a great singer's voice, though, and could do more with that in the future. In August 2015, she and Ari appeared together at a local coffee house "open-mic night," and performed their own beautiful, ocean-themed composition. This event later became a scene in an episode of *I Am Jazz*.[40.1] Since this was Jazz's first time singing in the spotlight, she was a bit nervous, but with practice, she could become an accomplished, confident vocalist like her sister.

Jazz loved her school acting classes, and once even attended a performance-art summer camp. She also participated in a number of school presentations of various kinds, mostly as a dancer. One acting class teacher stated that Jazz "has a wonderful energy. She is as brilliant onstage as off." [87]

The Art of Jazz

As do most children, Jazz began drawing when she was in preschool, but her artistic skills greatly improved with years of practice. She is a self-taught artist and admits to doodling some of her elaborate sketches during class time. On her family's TransKids Purple Rainbow website is a gallery of colorful illustrations Jazz has created from kindergarten to the present (Trans Kids Purple Rainbow.org). Comparing her beginning efforts to those done in fifth grade and on, there was a dramatic leap, from fairly good elementary-school drawing, up to that of a talented sketch artist. She was awarded an "honorable mention" in a 2012 citywide art contest for local students.

Jazz has stated about her art (or whatever projects she undertakes) that she is determined to practice and practice until she is satisfied with her technique.[48.1] She is a perfectionist by nature. Despite an extremely busy schedule, Jazz managed to hone her artistic skills in a remarkably short span of time, just two or three years from being an amateur to becoming an accomplished artist. That determination shines through to anyone viewing her latest black and white charcoal portraiture. Jazz even created an Instagram account to share some of her artwork (Instagram.com/jazz_artist). And now she is experimenting with an app to make fairy-tale pictures she calls *Whimsical Waters*, posted on another of her Instagram accounts (Instagram.com/Whimsical_Waters).

Wherever Jazz goes, she usually brings along a sketchbook she can pull out when there's a spare moment in the car or at school. She's constantly working on her drawings and technical skills. That often includes sketching different parts of the human form. One time she got in trouble at school for some drawings she made of breasts,[40.1] but her motivation is to improve her artistic skills, not to be provocative. A few of Jazz's striking, detailed depictions of people's eyes can be seen on her Jazz Artist Instagram page, and some of her portraiture has been posted to her Jazz Jennings Instagram account.

Besides drawing, Jazz has become skilled in the realm of arts and crafts. She's produced a few YouTube DIY videos. Viewers can learn to create their own beautiful "Jazzworks," using glass containers and seashells (YouTube–Jazz Jennings). It seems that whatever she puts her mind to creating, her combination of natural talent and diligent practice yield wonderful artistic results.

Mermaids are a frequent subject of Jazz's artwork, and when she was younger, her bedroom was crammed with mermaids in every form imaginable, covering the walls, shelves, and furniture. "They've been my favorite creatures for as long as I can remember."[62] Jazz so relates to these magical beings that she even nicknamed herself "Jazz Mergirl."

During some of her interviews, Jeanette Jennings has commented on this mermaid phenomenon, saying that, "All of the male-to-female younger transgender children are obsessed with mermaids. It's because of the ambiguous genitalia. There's nothing below the waist but a tail. And how appealing is that for somebody who doesn't like what's down there?"[94]

When she was about eight-years-old, Jazz began learning to cut and sew fabric to fashion her own mermaid tails for use in the family swimming pool. As time went by, she continued to improve her tail-making craft, and began selling a few of these homemade tails on an informal basis. Over the years, Jazz's tails have progressed *way* beyond the original amateur cloth versions, as she experimented with different materials, designs, and techniques.

Later on, it occurred to Jazz that she could sell these creations to raise funds for the TKPR Foundation. In 2013, she established a small, non-profit business named Purple Rainbow Tails (Purple Rainbow Tails.com). From the beginning of this business venture, Jazz has been assisted by her longtime friend Kaci.

Eventually, Jazz discovered it was necessary to purchase a special, very expensive grade of "platinum silicone" called "Dragon Skin" to obtain the best results for her customers. In addition, other specialized materials and tools were needed for her new enterprise. Because the startup costs were going to be beyond her means, this 13-year-old entrepreneur created an IndieGoGo online-fundraising campaign in November 2013. Donors were offered a variety of homemade gifts, depending on the amount of their contributions, which reached the $3,000 goal in just two months' time.[49]

With this new funding in place, Jazz could now proceed with product development, and begin producing custom-made, professional-quality mermaid tails. During the summer of 2014, while most other kids were enjoying a carefree vacation, Jazz was busy experimenting and perfecting her tail-making process. On her Purple Rainbow Tails business website, Jazz wrote:

> I'm very artistic, and put all my effort and soul into each tail. I'm one of those people that, when I'm not very good at something, I'll keep practicing and trying until it reaches my expectations (which are really high).[48.1]

Some of the techniques Jazz devised are proprietary, but on her website, and on her YouTube channel, she did explain the basic procedure. The first step is to meticulously glue together hundreds (Jazz says "millions") of small, circular, foam disks or "scales," to create a big "scale sheet." Liquid plastic is then poured over the sheet, and, when dry, the plastic sheet is peeled off of the foam. This plastic sheet becomes a reusable mold. The final step in the process is to pour liquid silicone onto the mold, and when that cures, pull the silicone scale "castings" out of the plastic mold.[40]

The final silicone sheet can then be cut to the correct shape, following different template patterns that Jazz designed herself. The tails are custom cut and assembled according to the detailed measurements and specifications each customer provides.

When the silicone construction stage is complete, Jazz then applies and blends beautiful silicone-compatible paint colors, using a compressed-air paint sprayer and paint brushes. She has become quite a skilled painter, and the results are stunning.[40]

The whole process of constructing, assembling, and painting these mermaid tails is a very time-consuming, detailed task, but Jazz is fortunate to have had a lot of help from "BFF" Kaci. On the Purple Rainbow Tails Facebook page, Jazz wrote, "I want to thank my best friend Kaci for giving an extra hand in this tail making process. I couldn't have done it without her!" [48]

Crafting these mermaid tails can take up to 30 hours of meticulous, skilled labor. That time factor, combined with the expensive materials required, produces tails that cost $600 apiece for a basic model, up to $2,500 for more-customized creations. However, compared to mermaid tails sold by other companies, Jazz's prices are actually quite competitive. Since the launching of her business in summer 2013, Purple Rainbow Tails has even filled a multi-tail purchase by a major Florida themed water park for use in some of their performances. Quite an accomplishment for a young teen.

In her *Q & A* YouTube video, Jazz said about making the mermaid tails, "I think my favorite part is just knowing that it will benefit other people, and that the money will go to the TransKids Purple Rainbow Foundation to help other transgender kids like me." [42] Jazz's company motto is, "With creativity and passion, I plan to change the world one tail at a time." [49]

Chapter 22

I Am Jazz – The Book

This chapter tells the story of a story, the children's picture book called *I Am Jazz*. What is this book all about, and why was it written? How was it conceived, authored, and published? Interviews with the authors, numerous articles and reviews, and pre-publication publicity answered these and other questions even before the book became available in September 2014.

The origin of *I Am Jazz* is rooted in the activism of two big-hearted and determined women, Jessica Herthel and Jeanette Jennings. Jessica is a graduate of Harvard Law School, but grew dissatisfied working as a lawyer. She was looking for something that would have more meaning for her.[101]

As a longtime ally of the LGBTQ community, Jessica had taught her three young daughters to be open-minded to diversity. However, the neighborhood school they attended was not a very diverse place, and provided little in the way of teaching children to be accepting of others who were different from themselves. So this activist mom decided to become involved with the local school district in support of diversity programs and training.[97 / 101] As Jessica tells it, "I met Jeanette while volunteering on a committee geared toward making schools safe for every child, and out of our friendship, this project (*I Am Jazz*) was born."[71]

Soon after they met in January 2013, Jessica learned from Jeanette that the *20/20* "Listening to Jazz" documentary would air on television in a few days. She recorded it to watch later.[29] Jessica's children, the youngest at four-years-old, became interested in Jazz Jennings when they came upon their mom watching the recorded program.[97] Instead of shooing them out of the room, Jessica decided to let her girls stay. Using kid-friendly terms, she explained what the documentary was about:

> Jazz has something special about her. She was born with a boy body. But that doesn't change the girl that she truly is on the inside. Her body got mixed up when she was growing in her mom's belly, and it came out in the shape of a boy, but that body isn't who Jazz is.[29]

After having this talk with her kids, Jessica wondered, "Could they really digest the meaning of transgender, when so many adults cannot?"[29] The answer would come in a few months, when the Herthel daughters met Jazz and her family.

Meanwhile, as Jeanette Jennings and Jessica Herthel were getting to know one another better, they discussed what it's like to parent a trans child, and how little most of the public understands about people who are transgender. In an interview she later gave to a reporter, Jessica related where this conversation led:

Jeanette and I began talking about the need for a tool that is very simple and straightforward, both for parents who consider themselves to be an ally and want their children to understand what transgender is, and also for schools that are encountering trans issues. We realized that there wasn't such a tool available for people who were having this conversation for the first time with kids, written in very simple terms.[97]

But what would that teaching tool be like? Jessica shared more of the publication's back story. It was spring 2013 when her children finally met Jazz. "We had gone to see Jazz appear in a school play. We went out for ice cream afterwards. The girls sat at a table giggling and talking."[101] When they visited the Jennings home, the younger girls "gleefully fell in line, following Jazz like ducklings up to her mermaid-adorned room, and it wasn't long before I heard the giggling of four little girls wafting down the hallway." [29]

The Herthel daughters had quickly accepted Jazz as just another one of the girls, and looked up to her as an older role model. They admired Jazz's beautiful hair, her cool clothes collection, and enjoyed making a funny video with her. Jessica later observed:

> They got it. Or at least, they got enough of it. I had told them that Jazz was a girl born with a boy body, and yet never once did it occur to my girls to refer to Jazz as *he*

or *him*. They saw Jazz for who she was on the inside: a bubbly, confident, girly girl." [29]

Once they got home that night, Jessica reflected about the evening:

> It's so easy. This was so easy for my little kids who don't know anything about anything. They don't know about hormones. They don't know about gender reassignment surgery.[101] Knowing someone who is transgender doesn't scare them, nor should it. They don't know about sex, and they don't need to, because transgender is about who a person *is*, not who a person wants to sleep with.[29]

After doing some more thinking on the visit with the Jennings family, it occurred to Jessica that a children's picture book about Jazz's story would be the perfect teaching tool she had been looking for.[71] The Jennings' early video recordings, the television documentaries, and Jazz's memories, would provide the material needed to write that story.

A book reviewer was interested to know why Jessica Herthel decided to write a picture book instead of something for older kids. The author's reply was that she wanted to provide an engaging resource that even parents of little kids could use as soon as their children were old enough to understand about people's diversity. "Jazz began self-identifying as a girl as soon as she learned to talk. Obviously, then, we can't wait until our children are in middle school to have this conversation." [71]

As Jeanette said about how other kids view Jazz, "She's still a human being. I'm hoping kids will embrace that. Let's get to them before they hear the negativity, and it won't be a big deal." [18] Jazz has a similar hope for the book's impact. "Children are more open to change than adults, so if the upcoming generation is okay with transgender people, then the world could change completely," she says.[84]

The storyline that Jessica planned was to have a six and seven-year-old Jazz be the first-person narrator, and tell about her early-life experiences and feelings. "We wanted it to be from the perspective of a very young trans kid, confident and comfortable with who she is." [29]

Young readers understand and relate to this story because it is presented from a child's point of view. The narrative tells how Jazz always felt different from other kids, and about her visit to the doctor that confirmed her strong sense of "being a girl inside a boy's body." *I Am Jazz* is the first children's book to mention the word *transgender*, and explain the meaning to its young readers. Jeanette told a TV reporter that, "It's the first of its kind. There's never been a little kid coming out and saying, 'Hey, I'm transgender, and it's okay.' " [78]

The memoir would go on to recount Jazz's struggles with inflexible grownups in school and in the youth soccer league, and how she ultimately gained the freedom to be her true self. This story is a lesson that the co-authors want to be heard not just by kids in the LGBTQ community, but by anyone who feels they don't fit in.

The point of *I Am Jazz*, as summarized by Jessica, is for children to "Speak your truth, be who you are, no matter what," and for parents to "Love the kid that you were given, not the kid you thought you were going to get." [97] It does not matter if this is a youngster coming out as being transgender or gay or anything else. "When a child speaks about something that is fundamental to who they are, adults and parents need to set aside their own issues and try to listen to what these children have to say."[97] That is the same message Jeanette Jennings has been expressing for years.

Speaking with a reporter from the *Houston Chronicle*, Jessica Herthel shared more of her hopes for what an effect *I Am Jazz* would have:

> If we can get the message out that it is possible for a child to identify as transgender from a very young age, that would be great. Part of the pushback we get is parents saying these children are too young to make this decision. I'm here to say to all parents of children two to four-years-old, this is not an act of rebellion. There's nothing political here. This is children looking in the mirror and telling parents who they see looking back. [18]

Jessica revealed that it took six different manuscripts before she got the story just right for its target audience, children in pre-school through third grade.[101] Her little girls were the perfect age to be a "focus group at home to help with revisions of the manuscript." Jazz and Jessica also wanted to reach several other types of readers as well: families with transgender children, other interested adults, including LGBTQ allies, teachers and school children, and communities coping with trans-related controversies, such as "bathroom-use laws." [71]

It's quite a challenge for any writer to reach so wide a range of readers, but first-time author Jessica Herthel succeeded in doing just that. Actor Laverne Cox said *I Am Jazz* is an "essential tool for parents and teachers," and that "I wish I had a book like this when I was a kid struggling with gender-identity questions." [97]

Discussing more about the process of writing Jazz's story, Jessica shared that she was advised by those in the children's book trade to write around a theme, like "Jazz Goes to the Zoo" or "Jazz Goes to the Movies." But the novice author wisely stuck to her instinct that the story "should be a proud, first-person introduction" to the life of a trans child, the main audience she and Jazz wanted to reach. [101]

Jeanette and Jessica figured that at best, the book might be taken on by a publisher specializing in material for the LGBT community. They also considered self-publishing, hired on a college art student to provide the illustrations, and Jessica thought printing 400 copies would be enough to get started.

Then fate stepped in. Jessica met someone who put her in touch with an influential figure in the Penguin publishing group, and that led to *I Am Jazz* being published within just a few months' time by Dial Books for Young Readers.[101] This was extraordinary, because such a fast-track to publication almost never occurs.

Once the final draft of the manuscript was accepted, Dial commissioned an experienced artist to provide pictures for the book. Shelagh McNicholas, who lives near Liverpool, England, is a well-known children's book illustrator who has an extensive portfolio of drawings done for a number of publishers. Her delicate and whimsical drawing style was a perfect match for *I Am Jazz*, and helped bring the story to life.

Describing her mixed-media technique, Shelagh (pronounced *She-luh*) explained that she first uses soft, number-3b artist pencils to sketch her drawings, and then applies the watercolors to fill in the illustrations. Her finished work is remarkably detailed and evocative, and could only come from someone with the heart of a child. Like Jessica Herthel, Shelagh says her own daughter Molly influences her work. "Once Molly was born, she became my real inspiration for picture books." [62]

According to Jessica, one significant challenge that faced Shelagh was how to illustrate the page where Jazz says, "I have a girl brain but a boy body."

> For weeks, I racked my brain as to how this could be effectively conveyed in a picture. But the hugely gifted Shelagh McNicholas took it in stride, with the brilliant

idea to illustrate the page by using real-life drawings that Jazz had made before, during, and after her transition.[71]

It required less than one-and-a-half years for *I Am Jazz* to get from conception to completion and publication. That's a surprisingly short turn-around time for a conventionally-published book. The copyright for the illustrations is held by the Penguin Publishing Group, while the copyright for the text belongs to the TransKids Purple Rainbow Foundation, which receives the royalties (profits) from the story.

A few months before *I Am Jazz* became available, a pre-publication listing appeared on Amazon.com. This was part of a publicity campaign to build interest ahead of the book's release, scheduled for September 4, 2014. In addition to Amazon.com, *I Am Jazz* was also offered by independent and chain bookstores such as Barnes and Noble and Books & Books in Florida.

The book's promotion continued on June 25, 2014, when Jazz gave a private reading before an enthusiastic crowd of invitees at the Care Resource Center in South Florida. Local *NBC Miami News* reporter Laura Rodriguez was on hand, and her two-minute report about *I Am Jazz* aired that night on the evening news. Jazz, Jessica, and Jeanette were interviewed. One older transgender attendee stated: "Jazz is an inspiration. She's a pioneer. She's going to break many, many barriers." Another trans adult added her observation about *I Am Jazz*, saying, "It's going to make a big difference, because in my day, there was none of this" available.[78]

Jazz's first official book signing was held on September 7 in a Fort Lauderdale Books & Books store, just after *I Am Jazz* became available for purchase. A number of these signings have taken place since that time, most-often in conjunction with Jazz's appearances at conferences and conventions around the US.

Irika Sargent, a journalist with *CBS Miami* television, put together a four-minute news piece centered around another bookstore signing event on September 21. She interviewed Jessica, Jeanette, and Jazz at the signing, and paid a visit to the Jennings' home to talk some more, and get a tour of Jazz's mermaid-filled bedroom. During her interview, Jessica Herthel summed up what *I Am Jazz* is all about: "We feel this message is universal," said the co-author. "It's about speaking your truth and not being ashamed about what makes you different." [82]

While these television news segments were limited to the South Florida region, Jazz and Jeanette next got to discuss *I Am Jazz* with a national audience. In late October 2014, they traveled to New York to speak with Katie Couric on her *Yahoo! News* Internet program. The eight-minute segment featured Jazz reading from her new book, and Katie used that as the starting point for the interview. Most of Katie's questions were similar to those asked by other journalists and reporters, except *I Am Jazz* was now center stage. [9]

One week later, ABC Fusion TV's Alicia Menendez came to the Jennings' home and spoke with Jazz, her parents, and both brothers. The news video ran for six minutes, and once again, *I Am Jazz* provided the framework for all of the questions. In her commentary, Alicia described Jazz as being "wise beyond her years," followed by Jazz expressing optimism that our society is heading in the right direction.

Using artistic metaphor, Jazz stated, "What I say is, people need to open their eyes and open their minds as well because right now the world is in black and white, and slowly people are beginning to create change. Color is beginning to come into this world, and I'm beginning to see tints and shades, so I am happy." [64]

What has been the impact of *I Am Jazz*? Since its September 2014 debut on Amazon.com, this children's picture book quickly climbed to first place in its special category, and was still number one when *Jazz Mergirl* went to print. Jessica Herthel and Jeanette Jennings saw their dreams come true when *I Am Jazz* became available in school libraries and classrooms across the country. In fact, just three months after the book's publication, Malcolm X Elementary in California put on an original play based on Jazz Jennings' story. Jazz videoed back a heartfelt "thank you" to the students for their moving performance.[46]

I Am Jazz has been widely-acclaimed by national book reviewers, countless readers, and well-known personalities. Besides actor Laverne Cox, television journalist Barbara Walters, trans-activist and author Janet Mock, famous fiction writer Jodi Picoult, and non-fiction author Brad Meltzer, have all given endorsements.[30]

About the book's impact, Jessica told *The Trans Advocate*:

We're starting to get feedback from families with trans kids, and the message we're getting is that when these kids read it, they feel joy. Not only does the book validate them – they now know they're not alone – but it also gives them language to explain what they're feeling. My hope is that this will help kids know that they're okay, and that they don't have to go through years of suffering.[97]

Chapter 23

Speaking of Jazz:
Recognitions, Awards, and Speeches

In her bedroom, Jazz has a shelf full of soccer trophies her teams have won, and now she can add cross-country track awards from school. Besides those accomplishments, Jazz has other recognitions she is even more proud of receiving. Her courage and advocacy on behalf of transgender youth have become widely-known within the LGBTQ community and beyond, and numerous acknowledgments have come her way. Barbara Walters observed, "Jazz is clearly making a difference and embracing the spotlight, advocating for transgender rights, receiving awards, posing on the red carpet, meeting stars." [95] The most prominent of these events are included in this chapter.

Jazz's first recognition of note was the prestigious "Colin Higgins Youth Courage Award," presented to her on June 25, 2012. This acknowledgment, and a monetary grant, is presented each year by the Trevor Project, a national advocacy group based in New York City. The award honors "ordinary yet remarkable individuals whose courage has helped to educate" the public about the LGBTQ experience. The Jennings family was present to watch 11-year-old Jazz receive her award, the youngest recipient ever. [53]

Speaking of Jazz

Afterward, Jazz Jennings gave her first significant talk, a three-minute, heartfelt speech before a ballroom full of about one thousand supporters, including many celebrities. Despite her young age, she confidently took to the speaker's podium, deftly adjusted the microphone, and read from the teleprompter like an experienced spokesperson. Jazz spoke with expression, in a poised and sincere manner, and paused for applause and for the laughter her good humor generated. These are all traits of a seasoned pro, which is quite impressive for such a young speaker.

All of Jazz's prior acting, singing, and dancing classes helped prepare her for this role as a public speaker. Jeanette Jennings is awed by her daughter's natural stage presence and self-confidence, saying she makes it look so easy. However, Jazz responds that speaking before such a crowd, including all those celebrities, is anything *but* easy.

In the closing words of her "Colin Higgins Award" acceptance speech, Jazz said:

> I have a motto. Everyone should be accepted for who
> they truly are. It makes me sad knowing that so many
> transgender kids are bullied, depressed, and suicidal,
> because they feel like they don't fit in. I want everyone
> to know, just because someone's brain doesn't match
> their body doesn't mean they're a freak, or a bad person.
> In fact, I think it means just the opposite. To me, kids

like us are unique and special, which I think is pretty
cool.[39]

Jazz then announced her intention to "pay it forward" by donating
the entire grant award to the TransKids Purple Rainbow Foundation. She
said her objective is to "try my best to help other kids be as happy as I
am right now." [39]

Several months later, in March 2013, the Jennings family was back
in New York to be honored by GLAAD (Gay and Lesbian Alliance
Against Defamation) at the organization's 24th "Annual Media Awards"
ceremony. One important topic highlighted that night was the problem of
discrimination against trans youth. An audience of over 3,000 gave the
Jennings a standing ovation for their advocacy on behalf of the LGBTQ
community.[53]

This appearance was the prelude to an even bigger event for Jazz
Jennings and her family. GLAAD had invited the now-12-year-old
spokesperson to represent the younger LGBT community at the Los
Angeles portion of this bi-coastal "Annual Media Awards" ceremony.
On Saturday evening, April 20, Jazz gave a three-minute speech before a
huge audience that included Hollywood stars and other famous
personalities. Actress Elle Fanning and *Glee*'s Alex Newell flanked Jazz
at the podium. "The trio spoke in support of LGBT youth and called for
more diversity and representation in the media." [17]

In her short but inspiring talk, Jazz was again poised and self-assured when she said:

> It's amazing to be here tonight, representing all LGBTQ kids and teens out there. I just want them to know that it's okay to step outside of your shadows and just be who you are. Just be true to yourself and express yourself, because after all, we are just kids, and all kids deserve to be happy.[17]

Afterward, former president Bill Clinton, daughter Chelsea, and actor Jennifer Lawrence asked to meet Jazz Jennings backstage. Jazz is never star-struck or overwhelmed by the famous people she often encounters. Nor does she flout "the fact that she has met them, or that framed photos of her posing with them hang on her walls at home."[84] In Jazz's view, they are influential voices that can help spread her message of equality and acceptance, and effect positive change. "They have a big voice in the world," she notes.[84]

Jazz also appreciates how much her own parents have done for her and on behalf of trans youth worldwide, including all of the work of the TKPR foundation that supports this community. So she was very pleased and proud that in June 2013, Greg and Jeanette Jennings were themselves honored with an "Equality Ally Award" given by Equality California. The Jennings family traveled to San Diego, California, for the award presentation.

Claire Stafford, a member of the Equality California host committee, presented the award to the Jennings, and in her remarks, talked about Jeanette and Greg's courage in standing up for Jazz and fighting for her rights. Claire observed, "That is what love and understanding is all about." [85]

When accepting this acknowledgment, Jeanette Jennings commented:

> It's such an honor to be here tonight receiving this 'Ally Award.' We have proudly watched Jazz receive her awards for her strength and incredible courage as an advocate for trans youth everywhere, and admit we are not accustomed to being the honorees. Greg and I are both humbled and are truly grateful for this recognition.[85]

Jeanette then called her three other children up on stage to join her, Greg, and Jazz. The family was given a standing ovation, which left Jeanette practically speechless. When she regained her composure, Jazz's mom briefly recounted the challenging pathway that had brought the family to this moment, and observed that it was Jazz's own "strength and tenacity that guided us through those early years." [85]

During Greg's portion of the acceptance remarks, he stated:

> We believe that it is a child's birthright to receive unconditional love from their parents. Even though we knew how cold and cruel the world could be, it never

occurred to us to force Jazz to conform to be somebody she clearly wasn't. So with love and support, we allowed her to socially transition. We knew the journey would be difficult, but we believed it was the right path for Jazz.

While on this journey, we also felt that it was important to share our story with others in the hope that we could raise awareness, educate others, increase tolerance, and effectuate positive change.[85]

Jeanette concluded the Jennings' joint speech by acknowledging those who came before, and created a pathway for them to follow.

We honor those brave individuals who shared their stories before us, gave us the knowledge and strength to do what we knew was right, and gave us the courage to share our own story, Jazz's story, with the world.[85]

Claire Stafford summed up the feelings of everyone present when she said to the Jennings family, "On behalf of all of us who have come before, and especially all the children and parents who have yet to face these gender issues, we wish to give you our heartfelt thanks for what you have done. We are all in your debt." [85]

One year later, in June 2014, the whole family returned to New York to see Jazz, the youngest at 13, and three young adults in their 20s, being presented with the Logo TV and Trevor Project's first annual "Youth Trailblazer Award." These honorees, including Jazz Jennings, were members of the Trevor Project's Youth Advisory Council, and were being recognized for making an impact in their communities. The one-hour, star-studded award ceremony was broadcast live on Logo Television.[59]

Logo TV had prepared a two-minute biographical documentary for each Trailblazer, all of which were combined into one abbreviated video for showing that evening. Each young Trailblazer was then introduced by actor Daniel Radcliffe. The complete two-minute documentaries were also shown on Logo TV in June.[59]

Jazz's video was a moving summary about her pioneering ways, and her message to be true to yourself and accept others for who they are. In this short film, Jazz explained to viewers, "I am different from other people because I am transgender, and that doesn't mean I am bad. It just means that I am different. Once I knew that other people couldn't live their lives as happy as I could, I knew that I had to help them." [59]

All of these awards, combined with numerous filmed appearances, the children's book *I Am Jazz*, and interviews in the media, raised the public's awareness of Jazz Jennings and her family's Purple Rainbow Foundation. Thus it was that her name and achievements came to the attention of *TIME* magazine.

TIME editors were quietly compiling a list of remarkable young people around the world that the magazine could honor. They "analyzed social-media followings, cultural accolades, business acumen, and more, to determine this list." [16] As the long roll of nominees was reduced down to a final select few, Jazz's name remained.

In October 2014, *TIME* announced its choices for the "Top 25 Most Influential Teens of 2014" world-wide, with Jazz among those selected for this recognition. Another prominent choice was Nobel prize-winner Malala Yousafzai, whom Jazz deeply admires. The magazine's recognition stated, "In a landmark year for transgender visibility in the media, Jazz Jennings stands out for how much she's already accomplished." [16]

When asked by a news reporter what her reaction was, Jeanette Jennings responded, "It's very surreal to see your child featured in *TIME* magazine, especially as one of the most influential teens in the world." [79] Jazz is almost always calm and self-controlled, but according to her mom, "With *TIME* magazine, she was screeching, 'Oh my goodness! I'm on the list with Malala!' She felt the company she was with, she was not worthy," Jeanette observed. "But she *is* worthy. To be compared in the same list as these people, it's extremely overwhelming for her, and she feels so flattered." [16]

In addition to this *TIME* magazine honor, Jazz Jennings became the youngest person to be chosen for *The Advocate* magazine's "Top 40 Under 40" list, the *Huffington Post* named her as one of the "14 Most Fearless Teens of 2014," and she was also selected for *Out Magazine's* "Top 100" list, and the "Trans 100 List for 2014." [53]

At the same time as "The Most Influential Teen" selections were being publicized by *TIME*, a press release was issued by Equality Florida stating that Jazz Jennings would be presented with the esteemed "Voice of Equality Award" for 2014. Equality Florida is an important LGBT civil rights group. Explaining why Jazz was selected to receive this honor, the organization's Deputy Director stated:

> This amazing young woman inspires us all with her courage and candor, demonstrating what is possible when we share our stories. We are proud to recognize her for the impact she already has made on the lives of transgender youth and their families here in Broward County and across the nation.[6]

When Jazz learned about being chosen for this recognition, she told a reporter:

> I feel so honored that Equality Florida selected me for their 'Voice of Equality Award.' This award shows me that I'm making a huge impact on others, and that I have to continue the work I'm doing, because sharing my voice really does affect other people.[55]

The gala award ceremony was held in Fort Lauderdale, Florida, in November 2014, and among the 500 attendees were Jazz's family and some of her friends. Also in attendance was Jazz's co-author, Jessica Herthel. Since the book *I Am Jazz* had just been published two months before, Jessica and Jazz planned to hold a book signing during the evening. Also, Jessica put on a "Go Fund Me" crowd-funding campaign to bring their book's wonderful illustrator Shelagh McNicholas over from England. Those donations enabled Shelagh to attend the award event, and she too autographed *I Am Jazz* for eager supporters.[7]

Most of Jazz's five-minute acceptance speech was dedicated to her message of accepting people who are different from themselves. One observation she made was received with both laughter and applause: "*Hello*! It's 2014! Different is the new normal!"[51] Speaking of her hopes and dreams for the future, Jazz once again relied on artistic metaphor to express herself:

> If we come together and get past our differences, then our world will begin evolving from black and white, and will transition into a beautiful place of colors, a rainbow of love, peace, freedom, and equality. I look forward to the day when being transgender is no big deal, and when all gender nonconforming people can feel loved and safe to be who they are.
>
> Progress is being made in our community, and the world is transitioning into a new time. As time moves on, I can see the change. I can see tints of color spreading throughout our society, and I know that one day, the world will be a beautiful place where the uniqueness and

diversity of each individual comes together to create the rainbow of equality.[51]

Just three months after her Equality Florida appearance, Jazz Jennings was once again called upon to be a spokesperson for the young transgender community. In mid-February 2015, she, along with her mom and Jessica Herthel, flew to Portland, Oregon, so Jazz could address the second annual Human Rights Campaign (HRC) "Time to Thrive" conference. HRC is the nation's largest LGBT civil rights organization, and Jazz had previously been selected as one of its Youth Ambassadors. She and other young people were chosen as HRC Ambassadors "because of their courage in sharing their own stories, and their demonstrated commitment to speaking out about issues facing all LGBTQ youth." [74]

According to the HRC website, the organization hosts this annual conference, along with the National Education Association and the American Counseling Association, "to promote safety, inclusion and well-being for LGBTQ youth everywhere." Conference attendees are primarily "youth-serving professionals, including K-12 educators, mental health providers, pediatricians, religious leaders, recreational athletic coaches, and youth development staff." [33]

Before Jazz came to the podium for her speech, another Youth Ambassador gave brief introductory remarks, and showed the audience a very compelling four-minute documentary assembled from numerous filmed pieces about Jazz Jennings and her family. Jazz's nine-minute speech followed, and was her longest and most impressive yet.[44]

In her talk, Jazz recalled her experiences as a young trans girl making her way through life. Much of this speech was devoted to sharing for the first time many details about the painful discrimination and struggles she had experienced as a student in preschool and elementary school. Jazz contrasted this situation with the much-improved conditions in middle school, where the administrators were accepting, very supportive, and quite protective.[44] A number of remarks from Jazz's speech are included in other chapters of this book.

In her concluding comments, Jazz addressed all of the education professionals in the audience, saying, "Gender nonconforming kids need adults like you to advocate for them. Every school district in the country should have a policy protecting kids like me." Citing the high-rate of suicide attempts by transgender youth, Jazz declared, "Each of you has the power to lower these statistics."[44] Jazz went on to exhort her listeners:

> When you have a student who is struggling with gender
> identity issues, be a mentor. Make them feel safe. Have
> an open-door policy. I'm only one person, but I'm here
> as a voice of trans youth everywhere. And by speaking
> today, my message will spread from you to others. That's
> why you have to do everything in your power to fight for
> our right to be treated equally, to be supported, and to be

respected for who we are. Knowing that at least one adult cares can make all the difference in the world to a transgender youth. Be that person. You can make a difference and change a life forever.[44]

As Jazz brought her speech to a close, it was not a surprise to onlookers when the audience rose to give her a standing ovation. That gesture was a show of admiration and respect for this inspiring 14-year-old girl.[44]

The awards and accolades keep on coming. At another gala event, in May 2015, Pride Center Fort Lauderdale and the Harvey Milk Foundation presented the new "Diversity Honors Award" to Jazz and a number of other honorees.[27] When giving her acceptance remarks from the large podium, Jazz suddenly appeared taller, wearing her stylish new high heels. Though still small in stature, her voice is anything but. Jazz's message of acceptance and understanding is spreading far beyond South Florida, to be heard nationwide, and even around the world.

An indicator of Jazz's increasing prominence as an advocate occurred when she and her parents were invited to a reception at the White House on June 24, 2015. The occasion was to celebrate LGBT Pride Month. The Jennings were present in the East Room when President Obama gave a speech to the invitees, and Jazz was interviewed in the West Wing near the famous Rose Garden. Her statement, and those of four other LGBT activists, were edited together and shared on a vlog posted to the White House Facebook page. In her remarks concerning the Supreme Court's pending ruling on same-sex marriage, Jazz said:

> Love is a beautiful thing, and we should just all embrace
> that and not judge people for who they want to love or
> who they want to be. I'm hoping in the future that people
> will look back at the civil rights movement of marriage
> equality and realize that it's just people being themselves
> and people loving each other for who they are, and it's
> not anything we should have made a big deal over.[45]

Those very same ideas could be expressed about the civil rights of transgender folks. In fact, Jazz's White House statement regarding civil rights brought her full-circle back to the May 2012 video message she sent President Obama asking that such rights be extended to people in the transgender community. Remarkable for a 14-and-a-half-year-old, much less a child aged 11 at that time.

In the words of the Florida Pride Center, their "Diversity Honor Awards" are given "to highlight those who have made a transformational effect on improving the lives of others, leading the change to promote inclusion and acceptance."[27] Jazz Jennings has done just that, and will continue doing so in the years to come.

*****

Despite all of the attention that Jazz receives, and the tributes and awards she is given, this young celebrity remains a very modest person.

In his TV interview with Jazz Jennings, Dr. Drew said to her, "You're ordinary in an extraordinary way," to which she replied, "Yes, that was perfect." [73] At the same time Jazz is becoming so well-known as an activist and spokesperson for transgender youth, she also wants to be known as a typical teen. Jazz says, I don't want to be labeled as 'the transgender girl.' I want to be called Jazz, the girl who just *happens* to be transgender.[92.1]

In another interview, Jazz summarized how she feels about herself and her role as an activist for transgender youth:

> Although everyone's compliments and messages of kindness are dear to my heart, I feel so humble. I'm just an ordinary kid. I just feel like me. I do what I believe is right to help others and spread my message. Being in the spotlight is critical because I know we are saving lives, and that's the greatest change I can be proud of.[71]

When she reached this point in the manuscript, one thoughtful 95-year-old lady shook her head in awe, and reflected, "Bruce Jenner – Caitlyn Jenner – just came out with a big splash, but this little girl Jazz, in her own quiet way, has been doing this, and more, for years now." Nearly every reader will be astonished after learning about Jazz's many accomplishments. These amount to more in her 14 years than most people realize in a lifetime.

However, all of this comes at a cost to Jazz, about which the reporter from *Cosmopolitan* magazine asked, "You're the face of trans teens, but do you have your moments where you get down, and if so, why?" Jazz's forthright reply is sobering. She said:

> For sure. I have so many moments where I feel really overwhelmed and stressed. So many people have expectations for me, look up to me, and I feel like I have the whole community riding on my back. Sometimes I wonder, 'Will things ever really get better? Can I actually make a difference?' So I have this hiding place where I kind of just sit alone, and I process everything.[81]

As she looks back over time, it is hoped that Jazz will gain a better perspective about what she has undertaken, and the accomplishments she has achieved. Maybe then this young but influential teen will realize what a difference – an incredible difference – she is making, and that things really *are* improving. Jeanette Jennings has observed that the world truly is a better place because of Jazz.

Chapter 24

Why Jazz?

It is remarkable that all of these accomplishments and tributes would be credited to any one person, especially someone as young as Jazz Jennings. Just how did that come to pass? If destiny plays a role, then Jazz is *not* just a happenstance. As her mom Jeanette said, "The journey we are on is the journey that's meant to be." [63]

Jazz came uniquely prepared for this journey. There is no better-equipped person to fill her position as a young pioneer and spokesperson for transgender youth. Jazz was born not with a "disorder," but rather as a "unique and special person," who came to this world with her own exceptional set of qualities, talents, and abilities. It doesn't hurt that she's so cute and has such an engaging personality.

It is the rare adult, much less a young teen, who could appear on television, or speak before a huge audience, or to a former president, with such poise, self-confidence, and charm. While doing so, Jazz is mature, wise, articulate, and inspiring. Even though she is often called upon to carry out some daunting task, she makes it all look so easy. But, of course, it's not.

When asked how she came to be so self-confident, Jazz said she was just born that way, but credited that strength to the encouragement and unconditional love she has received from her family.[77.1] "I think because my family has showered me with love and support right from the start, I've been able to display that confidence throughout my life."[40.1]

And what better family could Jazz ask for to help her along the challenging road she travels? Besides being an intelligent, open-minded, and very caring and encouraging father, Greg Jennings is an accomplished attorney. He's the perfect person Jazz needs to give her good counsel and guide her through the legal issues she encounters on her way. Jazz describes her dad as being "a wise, modest, kind, and serious man." [40.1]

Jeanette Jennings is an incredibly caring, loving, and supportive mother who always has Jazz's back. In addition, as a trained clinical counselor, Jeanette came especially ready to "navigate the uncharted territory" of having such a young transgender child. Jeanette says she follows her "gut feeling," and that has served Jazz so well. Much of the time, the Jennings have been on their own on this incredibly difficult journey, ably pioneering a path for other parents and their trans children.

Then there are Jazz's older sister and twin brothers, who, like their parents, are very caring and protective people. Yes, there are the occasional quarrels, as in any typical family, but Jazz's siblings have always been there to stand up for their little sister. Jazz says Ari is her role model. Being five-years-older, Ari was in the perfect position to help guide her sister through her early and middle school days. Ari promised she would be the best big sister, and has been just that. As the lead singer of a rock band, an activist, a student leader, and even the salutatorian for her high school's graduating class, Ari set an example for Jazz to follow. Now in college, she remains close to Jazz, and will continue being her role model.

In June 2015, Griffen shared that, "I'm going to be looking after Jazz a lot in high school. She might have a few bumps in the road because not everybody's accepting that she's transgender." [40.1] To which Sander added, "We're her brothers, and we will a*lways* be there for Jazz, no matter what the situation is." [40.1]

Jazz is also blessed with a set of loving and accepting best friends, some of whom have been with her since preschool days, through times both happy and sad. Jazz is especially fortunate to have Kaci as her BFF. Over the years, Kaci has given selflessly of her time and energy to help Jazz with many of her creative projects.

There would probably be no *I Am Jazz* book without Jessica Herthel having become friends with Jeanette, and Jessica's three daughters looking up to Jazz as a friend and role model. That's what led to the writing of such an influential, first-of-its-kind children's publication. It was through a chance meeting that Jessica was able to reach decision-makers within the publishing company, Penguin Group. Although this was her first time writing a book, Jessica had the natural talent and intuition that was needed to succeed with this challenging children's project. And, of course, she had a great story to work with.

Why Jazz?

Of critical importance to Jazz has been the healthcare team she relies on, which is made up of such caring professionals. Her gender therapist, Dr. Volker, has provided expert guidance and advice since Jazz was about three-years-old. The other members of Jazz's medical team, like her pediatric endocrinologists, have been equally knowledgeable, kind, and exceedingly helpful throughout the transition process. Jeanette told Dr. Drew how grateful she is that her family "landed in the hands of wonderful professionals." [73]

With all of her amazing qualities, and such a great support system in place, it's no wonder Jazz Jennings has found such success as an advocate for younger members of the LGBTQ community, and transgender youth in particular. Something to think about: Was it just a coincidence that Jazz came along so incredibly well-prepared and supported for her role in life? Or was this all, as her mom Jeanette said, destiny – a journey meant to be? [92.1]

Afterword
Probabilities and Possibilities

As this biography comes to a close, Jazz Jennings is just getting started. In her future, there are a number of events that will definitely take place, others that are likely to occur, and numerous paths that Jazz may choose to follow.

One significant event that just took place was for Jazz to move on to high school in August 2015, as *Jazz Mergirl* was being completed. Because the middle school shares the same campus with her new high school, Jazz thought this wouldn't be a dramatic change. However, she did express concerns about maybe not being accepted by the students there.[40.1] Since Jazz has already taken part in some of the varsity sports activities available to her while in middle school, that experience should help smooth her transition into the upper grades. Without doubt, Jazz will continue being active in the team sports that she enjoys, such as soccer, track, and tennis.

In her high school years, Jazz will be eligible to participate in a variety of student clubs and organizations that appeal to her many interests. The problem will be finding the time in her very busy schedule to participate in any extra-curricular activities. There are so many opportunities at her school that she might have difficulty selecting ones in which to take part, should she choose to do so. Here Jazz can find like-minded friends who will be accepting and supportive.

For instance, in addition to taking high school art classes, Jazz might join the art club, which produces paintings and sculptures for fundraising purposes. As well as fine art, Jazz is attracted to the performing arts. Although she no longer takes part in singing or dancing activities, Jazz still enjoys acting. If she had fewer outside obligations, she might have planned on becoming involved with the high school's junior thespian drama club that puts on theatrical performances. As it is, Jazz has been incredibly busy juggling her schoolwork and involvement in sports, while at the same time attending conferences, being interviewed, and filming her television docuseries, *I Am Jazz*. Those kinds of events will keep vying for a place on her calendar in the years to come.

Because she is so aware of the discrimination LGBTQ students frequently experience, Jazz intends on becoming involved with her high school's Gay-Straight Alliance.[*] This campus organization promotes tolerance and respect for all students, regardless of race, religion, social status, sexual orientation, or gender identity. As an activist and speaker for young members of the LGBTQ community, Jazz would be an asset to this group. But she also has to look at the bigger picture to decide how to best use her limited time, such as doing interviews and making appearances that will reach a national and international audience.

---

[*]Jazz's sister Ari was a member and president of this same campus group.

Despite her demanding schedule, this bright teen maintains an excellent academic record. In answer to one inquiry about her grades, she shared that, "I've never gotten lower than an A on my report card."[50] Jeanette explained more about Jazz's academic achievements: "She's always been such an amazing student. The child's never seen a B in her entire life. She's a perfectionist. Not only does she want straight A's. She wants 100 in every class." [8.1]

In middle school, Jazz was proud to qualify for the Jr. National Honor Society, and will be recognized by the high school's Honor Society too, provided she keeps up her grades. That might be a challenge though, with all those additional responsibilities Jazz has going on in her life. In this same regard, her high school includes a group affiliated with the Miami Herald Silver Knight Awards, one of the nation's most highly-regarded student recognitions. This award honors students who have earned both good grades *and* selflessly volunteered their talents and specialized knowledge in noteworthy service to their schools and communities. When she is in 12th grade, Jazz will definitely be eligible for consideration by this organization. It is a distinct honor just to be nominated for this award, and Jazz has an excellent chance of being selected.[*]

Another definite milestone will be Jazz's high school graduation, which will occur in early June 2019, and she plans on attending college after that. Since Jazz is just beginning high school, she told a reporter

---

[*]Ari was also in the National Honor Society throughout her high school years, and was nominated for the Silver Knight Award in 2014.

that she really hasn't thought much about higher education, and semi-jokingly said, "I'll probably just go to Harvard!" But then Jazz told the reporter, "One of my teachers was like, 'You're on *TIME* magazine's *Top 25 Most Influential Teens*? You could get into any college!' "[81] With Jazz's excellent academic record, well-rounded student activities, and her incredible accomplishments, her teacher is absolutely correct.

However, before moving on to higher education, it is very possible that Jazz will seek some form of *surgical transitioning*. Since 18 is the adult "age of consent" required by surgeons for this type of operation, trans students often have these procedures done between graduating high school and entering college. Then again, since a few doctors are now performing some transition surgeries on patients younger than 18 (see Chapter 18), it may turn out that the timeline for Jazz will be speeded up.

Regarding this subject, a reporter asked Jazz, "Are you thinking about the medical changes you may or may not make?" She responded:

> I'm still so young, but the gender reassignment surgery is definitely something I've been considering because it's really the next big step in my transition. I'm not like, 'I need to do it right away.' It's a big deal. You're really changing your body, so it's something I really have to think about.[81]

As was explained in a previous chapter, opting for surgery is a most personal decision, one that will vary from person to person. Jazz will need to wait and see how her body responds to hormone therapy, and how she feels about her gender presentation (appearance) when she becomes old enough. Again, this is a decision Jazz, her parents, and physicians will need to figure out when the time comes. She has expressed gender dysphoria since about the age of two, so a decision to undergo gender-confirmation surgery seems quite possible. If need be, Jazz can also seek guidance from her gender therapist as she makes this momentous choice.

What might be expected of Jazz Jennings in college and beyond? Jazz recently wrote about her plans for the future that she is considering a number of possibilities: "I want to be a scientist, a writer, I want to make movies, and I want to be an artist." [50]

Chances are Jazz will find career opportunities in a field related to her interests and passions, such as fine arts. So in college, perhaps she will pursue a theater arts major, and go on to a career in television or film. After all, she has already become a star on her own television series. On a Twitter post in June 2015, she wrote: "I love to write and come up with creative stories! Therefore I want to be a writer or film maker.[*] I like TV movies more though."[47] Or Jazz might decide to study more in the visual arts, and become a professional artist.

Yet, Jazz is a well-rounded student with a wide-range of interests and abilities. In another recent Twitter post, she wrote, "I LOVE math and science and definitely want to explore the different fields in the

_____

[*]Following college, Jazz's mom was also involved in the film business.

industry sometime in the future." [47] Possibly she will choose to focus on a career in a scientific field, or maybe get into gender studies or psychology, in preparation for becoming a gender therapist or other type of counselor.[*]

Besides education and career-readiness, Jazz has many other activities and projects that attract her attention. One possibility for her is to produce more written and videotaped materials. Since the autobiographical children's picture book *I Am Jazz* has been published to wide-acclaim, Jazz may someday decide to write a follow-up autobiography for teen readers, like the recently published books *Rethinking Normal* (Katie Rain Hill), *Some Assembly Required* (Arin Andrews), and the biography *Becoming Nicole*, the story of Nicole Maines (Amy Nutt).[†]

In recent years, Jazz has become recognized as a spokesperson and activist for transgender youth and for the younger LGBTQ community as a whole. Undoubtedly she will be called upon more often to speak out for the rights of the young people within that population. There will be more televised appearances, online discussions, and interviews with magazines and other news media. And, of course, Jazz will keep on

---

[*]If Jazz were to enter the helping professions, maybe as a counselor, she would be following in her mom's footsteps, since some years ago Jeanette worked in clinical counseling.

[†]Perhaps Jeanette, who keeps a journal regarding the Jennings' experiences, will some day write *her own* memoir about raising Jazz and becoming an advocate for transgender youth.

speaking before large audiences at conferences and award presentations. In a June 2015 interview with *Cosmopolitan* magazine, Jazz stated:

> I really want to continue being an activist. I always say that I want to leave this world in a better state than when I arrived, and the only way that's going to happen is if I continue moving forward until I see the change that I want to see.[81]

With that goal in mind, Jazz Jennings might follow the example of other well-known transgender activists, and write some editorials to be distributed online and in the print media. Or she might produce more of her own YouTube video messages (vlogs).

One particular area this young activist could focus on is unfair laws and restrictions that affect the transgender population in her own state of Florida. Jazz may initiate a challenge to those discriminatory practices, as she and her parents did during her elementary school years. Jazz and Jeanette have already voiced opposition to so-called "bathroom bills," which are laws that prohibit transgender individuals from using restrooms of their affirmed gender.*

Another option for Jazz to consider would be confronting the outdated requirement in Florida that sex-reassignment surgery be performed *before* transgender individuals can change the gender

---

*The Florida state senator who proposed such a law was satirized in the press as "wanting to put Jazz Jennings in jail." [40.1]

designation on their birth certificates. That's a law just waiting to be revised.

As her videography skills continue to grow, Jazz is sure to create other YouTube projects besides the serious messages. Since she loves doing arts and crafts, she plans on posting new DIY instruction videos. Her many fans keep asking for more of these uploads. Also, Jazz may produce additional humorous and entertaining recordings, like the *Bloopers* episodes.

If her past is any indication, Jazz will keep on improving as an artist, and might explore other creative outlets. And it's possible she will expand her Rainbow Tails business venture, or maybe find other artistic fundraising endeavors to benefit her family's TransKids Purple Rainbow Foundation. One great fundraiser would be for Jazz to sell autographed originals and prints of her amazing artwork. (This author would like one of those!) Later on, if her schedule permits, perhaps Jazz will become more involved with the daily operations of the TKPR foundation. As this organization expands, and the workload increases, her mom will need more help.

*****

With all of her talents and abilities, and her dedication and resolve, Jazz's ongoing journey is rich with promise and possibility. As that pathway goes forward, only time will tell for sure where it leads her, but Jazz does have many ideas. In a 2014 speech, she declared: "I have accomplished so much in the process of spreading this message of equality, but, compared to the plans I have in mind, there is still so much more to do!" [51] And Jazz recently wrote: "I just want to live life to the fullest and change the world!" [50]

Whatever the future holds for Jazz Mergirl, it is sure to be a fascinating, exciting, often moving, and quite inspirational journey of courage, determination, and love. To be continued …

"I am Jazz. I love saying that."

~Jazz Mergirl~

Appendix 1

Jazz's Notable Quotes

From Dr. Seuss: Be who you are, and say what you feel, because those who mind don't matter, and those who matter don't mind!

On the *I Am Jazz* OWN documentary, Jazz observed: I say a lot of things are *amazing* because a lot of things *are*! [87]

Commenting on when her parents were told the doctor's diagnosis of gender dysphoria: At that time, they had *no idea* the adventure they were about to embark upon!

About other peoples' criticisms: I know that they don't determine who I am – I decide. I have the right to make my own decisions, whether people respect it or not. Being transgender makes you a stronger person. The challenges you overcome help you better understand yourself and the world around you.[71]

I would *not* wish to *not* be transgender, 'cause I like the way I am. It's the person I am. And I'm proud of myself and what I've accomplished. It's made me a braver person, being transgender. And it's just become a part of me.[68]

You just have to be proud of who you are and have confidence, because you are beautiful no matter what.[82]

On her self-confidence, Jazz and Jeanette said on BuzzFeed:

Jazz: Without your love and support I wouldn't have discovered my confidence!
Jeanette: I think that even if you weren't born transgender, you really are just a confident person.
Jazz: Just take the credit. You are an amazing mom!

I have to love myself. I just have to be happy with who I am. That's all that matters.[10]

I'm only friends with the people who will accept me for my true heart no matter what.[71]

Question: Do you identify more as trans or more as a girl?
Answer: As Jazz.[50]

I don't want to be labeled as 'the transgender girl.' I want to be called Jazz, the girl who just *happens* to be transgender.[92.1]

I am a soccer player. I am an artist. I am a high schooler. I am transgender. I am proud. I am Jazz! (Instagram).

I'm proud of the way I am, and I wish all transgender kids could embrace their uniqueness like I do. I share my stories so that my message of loving yourself and knowing it's okay to be different can be spread everywhere.[44]

Advice for other transgender kids: Just always stay true to yourself no matter what. Express your inner emotions, and don't let others tell you who you are. If your parents are not supportive, find a friend or adult who is. Let them guide you and help you open up. Let your feelings blossom, and keep growing. Don't let the opinions of others make you shrivel, for you are a beautiful person no matter what anyone says. Be the beautiful flower you are.[71]

From Jazz's "Young Trailblazer Awards" video: I am different from other people because I am transgender, and that doesn't mean I am bad.

It just means that I am different. Once I knew that other people couldn't live their lives as happy as I could, I knew that I had to help them.[59]

About writing *I Am Jazz*: I hope this book will help others to be who they are and stay true to themselves. I want this book to educate kids about what transgender means and that being different is okay. This way if they ever meet a kid like me, they will learn to accept them and love them for their personality. This book was created to help others, and that's what I hope it does.[71]

Although everyone's compliments and messages of kindness are dear to my heart, I feel so humble. I'm just an ordinary kid. I just feel like me. I do what I believe is right to help others and spread my message. Being in the spotlight is critical because I know we are saving lives, and that's the greatest change I can be proud of.[71]

On the *I Am Jazz* OWN documentary, she commented about going with her mom to panel discussions: I love inspiring people when I go on the panels. And I love when they say that I'm doing the right thing.[87]

Dr. Drew to Jazz: "You're ordinary in an extraordinary way," to which Jazz replied, "Yes, that was perfect." [73]

I don't mind being different. Different is special! I think what matters most is what a person is like inside. And inside, I am happy. I am Jazz.[30]

In being different, there is no right side or wrong. It's just who you are.[41]

Voice of Equality Award acceptance speech: *Hello*! It's 2014! Different is the new normal! [51]

I want to see every person have the freedom to be whoever they are.[68]

People think 'black and white.' They don't see the rainbow in the world. It's really just closed-minded.[9]

Quote from Jazz's "Voice of Equality Award" acceptance speech:

> If we come together and get past our differences, then
> our world will begin evolving from black and white, and
> will transition into a beautiful place of colors, a rainbow
> of love, peace, freedom, and equality. I look forward to
> the day when being transgender is no big deal, and when
> all gender nonconforming people can feel loved and safe
> to be who they are.
>
> Progress is being made in our community, and the world
> is transitioning into a new time. As time moves on, I can
> see the change. I can see tints of color spreading
> throughout our society, and I know that one day, the
> world will be a beautiful place where the uniqueness and
> diversity of each individual comes together to create the
> rainbow of equality.[51]

Speaking about the changing word: I always say that I want to leave this
world in a better state than when I arrived, and the only way that's going
to happen is if I continue moving forward until I see the change that I
want to see.[81]

Referring to the fact that many cisgender people are so focused on
transgender anatomy: Gender is so much bigger than that. It's like,
'Don't judge a book by their cover, and don't judge people by their
genitals.'[81]

*****

Greg Jennings: We live and we learn along *with* Jazz. There's going to
be some rocky roads, and we're going to stick together.[40.1]

Jeanette Jennings: No blurred TV faces for us. We are out, we are proud,
and we will continue to spread our message of unconditional love.[35]

Appendix 2

Q & A about Jazz

ORIGINS

What was your birth name (boy name), what is your real last name, where do you live, and what school do you go to? "I don't share this information because it's personal and could reveal my identity to certain people. It's for my safety." [43]

In July 2015, Jazz's dad Greg shared with a TV interviewer that Jazz's birth name was Jaron. [40.1]

SOCIAL

Do you have a Twitter account and other social media accounts?

Facebook pages are: Jazz Jennings–Public Figure, I Am Jazz–TV Show, and Jazzmergirl–Purple Rainbow Tails.

Google+ is Jazz Jennings (IAmJazz).

Instagram accounts are JazzJennings_, JazzTransgender, IAmJazzTrans, Jazz_Artist, Whimsical_Waters, and PurpleRainbowTails.

Kik is iamjazz2.

Snapchat is jazzmergirl.

Twitter is JazzJennings_.

Vine is JazzTransgender.

YouTube channel is Jazz Jennings.

Will you follow me? Jazz did try following people on Instagram for a time, one person per week, but it just got to be too much for her to keep up with. She already has an extremely busy schedule. There's school, sports, her cable television series, making mermaid tails for the foundation, and going to appearances around the country. So, following her close friends and relatives is pretty much the limit.

Will you write back to me? See previous answer.

What's your phone number? "I'm sorry ☹ I don't give out my phone number for my personal safety and privacy." [42]

Do you like boys? "Yes, I am attracted to boys." [95] But Jazz also says she relates to the idea of being *pansexual*, meaning she is attracted to people for their personality rather than their gender.

Have you ever been on a date, have a boyfriend? Briefly in fifth grade. [50]

How do you feel about being famous? Jazz told Oprah on *Where Are They Now?* "I've discovered that it's not about *me*, but more of my message. So, I don't care about the fame. I don't care how people treat me. I care about my message living on through other people."

PHYSICAL

People can ask very intrusive, personal questions that they themselves would never agree to answer, like, "What's in your pants?" But Jazz has been remarkably open and patient about answering many of those questions because she is so determined to educate and spread acceptance and understanding.

Are you going to get female hormones? Jazz has been taking these since 2013.

Do you still have boy parts? Yes.

Are you going to get gender reassignment surgery? Jazz responds that this is a private, very personal matter. Anyway, she does not know for sure yet. It's a major, life-changing decision. Jazz needs to think a lot more about this choice and see how she feels when a little older.[50/80/64.1]

You look very petite. What's your height and weight? 5 feet, 3½ inches, and 115 pounds.[50]

LIFESTYLE

Do you use makeup? Sometimes Jazz does use makeup, when having fun with her friends, or when she appears on camera, but most of the time, nothing except "Baby Lips" lip gloss, and "Clean and Clear" skincare. "I guess you can say my signature look is, beauty comes from within, because that's what I believe in." [58]

Do you ask your parents to buy you a lot of stuff? To one interviewer, Jazz said she usually does not ask her parents to get her a lot of things, although she knows many other teens do so. As it is, Jazz is very grateful for what she has, and for all her mom and dad do for her. However, because of all her appearances on TV and other media, Jazz has lately been adding to her wardrobe.

When I see your YouTube videos, your bedroom always looks so neat and organized. Are you that way all the time? Jazz is very organized about the things that are important to her. But she admits her mom is always after her to clean up her messy bedroom. "She calls me a slob all the time … Yes, I *am* a slob." [81] Jazz says one of her current goals is to get her room and work areas better-organized.[40.1]

LIKES AND INTERESTS

Mermaids: "They've been my favorite creatures for as long as I can remember." [82] Jazz so relates to these magical beings that she even nicknamed herself "Jazz Mergirl."

Talent: "I love sports, acting, and art. I also used to do singing and dancing."

Favorite activities: "I am a typical 14-year-old girl. I love to hang out with my friends. I love to play soccer and tennis, draw, and write stories, make silicone mermaid tails, and most of all, I *love* to binge-watch TV shows on my laptop." [44]

Music: Jazz enjoys *all* kinds of music. (An old favorite song from childhood is "Mamma Mia" by Abba.)

Favorite genre of books: Sci fi / fantasy.

Reading: "I love manga and anime." [50]

Favorite anime: "I love anime! My favorites are: *Avatar – The Last Air Bender*, *Legend of Korra*, *Fairy Tail*, *One Piece*, and *Code Geass*." [50]

Favorite TV series: *Game of Thrones* (HBO), especially Emilia Clarke, *The Walking Dead*, reality programs like *Big Brother*, *Survivor*, *Amazing Race*, *Celebrity Rehab*, and *Jersey Shore*.[50] (And now she can add the TV docuseries *I Am Jazz*.)

> Jazz's favorite TV series as a child were *H2O: Just Add Water* and *Hannah Montana*.

Favorite movies: "My favorite is action / sci fi. I have a few favorite movies, but I really love *Inception*, *Lord of the Rings*, and *Star Wars*." Jazz also likes *Avatar*.[50]

Favorite Disney movies: *Beauty and the Beast, Little Mermaid,* and *Lion King.*[50]

Favorite colors: When younger, her favorites, in order, were, "First is pink, second is silver, and third is green." [30] Today Jazz's favorite color is aqua, the color on her bedroom walls.

Favorite food: One is chocolate milk or shakes, and another is cheese burgers. Jazz admits she is not the healthiest eater.

Future work (answer when age 7): "I'd like to be a soccer player, an actress, singer, and dancer, maybe an artist, a lot of things!" [28]

Future work (answer when age 14): "Many things. I want to be a scientist, writer, I want to make movies, and I want to be an artist. I just want to live life to the fullest and change the world." [50]

> On her Twitter page, she posted, "I love to write and come up with creative stories! Therefore I want to be a writer or film maker. I like TV / movies more though." [47]
>
> Jazz recently stated, "I really want to continue being an activist," working to bring about change for the LGBTQ community.[81]

Most-disliked thing: "I don't know why, but I really hate lizards!" [50]

If you were the queen of the whole world for one day, what would you do? "Freedom and peace for all, and then do really fun things!" [50]

Who are your heroes? "My family." [50]

~~Jazz Mergirl~

Appendix 3

Questions for Discussion

Inspired by and adapted from
"A Reader's Guide" from *Raising My Rainbow*,
Copyright © 2013, by Lori Duron.

1. Do you believe that a person's *gender identity* and *gender expression* are more the result of *nature* (it's just how we were born), or *nurture* (what we learn from our family and society), or some combination of the two?

2. Is it acceptable for a birth-assigned male to identify as a female, or for a birth-assigned female to identify as a male?

3. If you were the parent of a daughter who wanted to wear stereotypical boy-type clothes for school, would you allow that? What about a son who wants to wear a dress to school?

4. Why do so many people in our society seem to be more comfortable about and accepting of a girl expressing herself in male ways (a "tomboy") as compared with people who are often not accepting of boys expressing themselves in more effeminate ways ("sissy boy")?

5. Is it important for the parents of an LGBTQ child to consider what other people might think or say about how they raise their child?

6. If parents *do* allow society to influence their child-raising decisions, and encourage their child to conform to society's expectations of what is "conventional," are they doing that to avoid being judged, talked about, and pressured? Or to save their child from harassment and bullying?

7. Would forcing a transgender or gender nonconforming (gender-expansive) child to conform to society's expectations really protect that child?

8. Is it best for a person who is LGBTQ to be recognized by their family when very young, or later on in their life?

9. Do you think there will ever be a time when people won't have to go through a "coming out process," but instead will be allowed by society to just be who they identify as?

10. As a parent, would you teach your children to be empathetic to others who are different from themselves? What would you expect their response to be when they see someone appearing in *any way* to be different from the way most people appear?

11. Before a child is even old enough to know or express their gender identity, should parents treat their child based on their birth-assigned gender, boy or girl? (For example, stereotypical pink for girls, blue for boys.) Or should parents not make assumptions?

12. If you knew someone who was LGB, how would you feel about that person and their family? Sad, happy, upset, antagonistic, supportive? Why?

13. What if someone you know came out as transgender, gender nonconforming (gender expansive), or agender? Would your response be different than if the person identified as gay or lesbian? Why or why not?

14. How would members of *your own* family react if they found out you or another family member were LGBTQ? Are there some who would be more accepting than others? What would *you* do if some people in the family were not accepting and supportive?

15. What impact, if any, do you think religion has had on establishing and maintaining our society's expectations as to what is considered acceptable and "normal" gender-related expression and behavior?

16. Do you think gender is limited to being "binary," only male and female, or are there shades of variation in between?

17. If you agree there is a "gender spectrum," ranging from male to female, and "shades of the rainbow" in between, where do you see yourself? Have you always viewed yourself that way, or has your gender identity and / or sexual orientation changed over time?

18. Did reading *Jazz Mergirl* affect your thinking about your gender identity and / or sexual orientation? If so, in what ways?

~Jazz Mergirl~

Appendix 4

What I'd Like You to Know

Inspired by: "Tips for Talking with a Transgender or Gender Nonconforming Person," from *Transgender Explained*, Copyright © 2009 by Joanne Herman, "Twelve Things Every Gender-Nonconforming Child Wants You to Know," from *Raising My Rainbow*, Copyright © 2013 by Lori Duron, "How to Talk to Your New Transgender Friend," from *Some Assembly Required*, Copyright © 2014 by Arin Andrews, "Tips for Talking to Transgender People," from *Rethinking Normal*, Copyright © 2014 by Katie Rain Hill, and the latest, "10 Things You Need to Know About Transgender People," by Jazz Jennings, © CosmopolitanOnline.com, and YouTube, June 8, 2015.

That you have read *Jazz Mergirl* suggests you already knew, or now know, about the important thoughts shared below. By educating yourself and sharing this information with others, you will help open minds and hearts and make the world a safer, more accepting, and supportive place for transgender people everywhere.

Each transgender person has their own road to travel, but there are some fundamental, widely-held truths and concepts with which many in this community will agree. While the following is given in the form of a "first-person" presentation, all of these ideas were actually inspired by the various resources cited above.

1. Most people are born with their body's sex matching up with the gender identity in their brain. For me, being transgender means my body's birth-assigned sex does *not* conform to my internal, deeply-held gender identity in my brain.

2. And despite what many people believe, most kids, whether conventional gender or transgender, know from an early age what their gender identity is. Between the ages of 15 months to two-years-old, children begin naturally gravitating to stereotypical girl or boy-type toys, clothing, and other forms of self-expression, and relate to the male or female role models all around them.

3. Please don't inquire about my birth name or ask what my "real" name is. The chosen name I go by *is* my real name. When referring to the past, I still ask that you go by the name I use now.

4. The same applies for using the pronouns to which I relate. My pronouns are an integral part of my internal identity. If you make a mistake about this, or anything else, just correct yourself, and move on. What matters most to me is that you are trying your best to be respectful, accepting, and understanding. If you aren't sure what my pronoun is, then just quietly ask me.

5. I say, "Quietly ask," because it is quite important for my safety to be cautious about sharing that I am transgender. Also, just because I've shared with you, or I am "out," does not mean I want you to be the one to spread around such personal information about me. Please respect my privacy by keeping this knowledge confidential, and allow me to determine who knows what and when.

6. Don't ask me about my anatomy. You wouldn't want someone asking, "What's in *your* pants?" There's a reason they are called "private parts," because they are … private. By the way, an estimated two-thirds of all trans individuals never do seek gender-affirming surgery, either because they don't choose those procedures, or because they cannot afford the steep cost involved.

7. When getting to know me, it's okay to ask if I'm open to discussing my past or my transition. However, be aware that many trans individuals choose to put the past behind them and don't wish to talk about it. They just want to get on with their lives. Respect whatever boundaries we set, and for sure, do not ask intrusive questions about intimate subjects such as hormones and surgeries.

8. Despite a widespread misunderstanding, trans people are not all gay! Far from it. Know that my internal, deeply-held gender identity is not directly related to my sexual orientation (sexual attraction). A transgender person, just like a cisgender (non-trans) individual, may be straight, gay, bi, or "none-of-the-above."

9. Be thoughtful with your words. Use the term "transgender" as an adjective, such as "transgender man," or "trans woman." Don't use "transgenders" or "a transgender," like a noun.

10. Don't say "transgendered" like a verb, which is akin to saying someone is "gayed" or "lesbianed." And please do not refer to "transgenderism," which makes it sound like I have a disease.

11. Never call me a "he-she," "it," "freak," "tranny," or any of the other derogatory, hate-based descriptors out there. Not only are these

words terribly offensive, they just amplify a trans person's sense of not belonging.

12. On the other hand, difficult as this may be, I do try to ignore such hatred when it's directed at me, and get on with my life. People who say those odious things are simply displaying their inhumanity and ignorance.

13. Treat me the same way you would want to be treated, as a decent human being. While I may in some ways be different from most of the people you know, different is not evil or bad. It's just ... different. Like you, I deserve to be accepted and given the same respect and rights as everyone else.

14. Did you know that the transgender population has the highest rate of self-harm and attempted suicides of any group on Earth? The main cause of this dire situation is the lack of support and unconditional love from many of our families, and / or the rejection and hate we often experience from the communities within which we live, attend school, and work.

15. Be open-minded to people who may be unlike yourself. Ignorance leads to fear of the unknown, and that causes people to reject and even detest those like me whom they do not know or understand. Make an effort to become a more informed person. Watch some of the Jazz Jennings videos on YouTube. As Jazz says, "Get to know us. You'll love us!"

16. Every transgender person is as different and unique as any other person. So each one of us will have a different and unique experience along the way. Please respect my own distinct wants and needs about my transition, and be patient, kind, accepting, and understanding of the very challenging road I travel.

17. Finally, again quoting Jazz: "Being transgender is something I embrace and am proud of, and it's a part of me. But I want people to know that there's *so* much more to me than that!" [40.1]

~Jazz Mergirl~

Appendix 5
Advice for Educators

In March 2015, Jazz Jennings spoke before the Human Rights Convention's "Time to Thrive" conference. In her keynote speech, she directed her remarks to the teachers, administrators, counselors, and other education professionals in attendance.

Jazz first told the conference audience about the difficult time she experienced as a transgender student in elementary school (until fifth grade), and contrasted that with her far-more positive middle-school experience. The remarkable difference, Jazz explained, was primarily due to the way she was treated by school administrators, and the school atmosphere they promulgated. She then exhorted conference attendees to use their influential positions to effect positive change for LGBTQ students within their own schools.

It is in this same spirit that the following recommendations are presented for principals, teachers, and counselors to consider for implementation. This is largely based on the author's own years as a classroom teacher and facilitator, working with young and older students, as well as adults. Additional inspiration came from "Tips for Educators" in Lori Duron's *Raising My Rainbow*.

Advice for Educators

1. Within your schools and classrooms, establish a climate of treating others with dignity and respect. Model that behavior yourself. Cultivate in your students an attitude of acceptance and open-mindedness to those who may be different from the majority. Make it your policy to promptly address instances of name-calling or bullying, either doing so in a private, one-on-one fashion, or with the whole class, whichever is more appropriate.

2. See each student as a unique and special person, deserving of our empathy and equal treatment, whatever their differences. Teach that same outlook to your students. Here is an example of putting this recommendation into practice:

Jacque Nunez is a Native-American storyteller and performer who conducts interactive school assemblies. She incorporates into her presentations a lesson about treating others with respect, regardless of differences. Jacque explains how her own children, dressed in authentic Indian clothing, had been ridiculed when attending some previous assemblies with her. They were reluctant to appear with her again.

That is how Jacque came to learn from a child psychologist friend how children tend to laugh at and make fun of people and things that are new and unusual for them. This simply arises out of their discomfort and lack of understanding and tolerance.

After explaining all of this to the assembled students, Jacque teaches them how to deal with that uneasiness in a more productive and caring manner, instead of laughing, as many are inclined to do. It's easy, she says. When you encounter someone who is unlike yourself, practice the habit of touching your finger to your cheek, and thinking, "Hmm. That's different." This is an effective technique that breaks the cycle of discomfort and laughter, and opens up the mind to be receptive to new and unusual experiences. It really does work.

3. When working with students in your classroom and around the school campus, strive to be as gender-neutral as possible. For instance, instead of saying *boys and girls*, address them as *class*, *scholars*, *students*, *people*, *friends*, and so forth.

4. During lessons and class discussions, especially in reference to job and career titles, use gender-neutral terms. Examples: police officer instead of policeman, firefighter in place of fireman, service person in place of serviceman, humankind instead of mankind. Post pictures of women doing work stereotypically associated with men, such as being a scientist, doctor, or other professional, auto repair specialist, military service person, information technologist, and so on. Do the same for men working in occupations often thought of as being mostly for women, such as an elementary school teacher or nurse.

5. When dividing students into groups, never do so by the "boy-girl" method, such as boy vs. girl teams or girl's lines and boy's lines. Constantly mix student groupings and partner work.

6. Speaking of teams, make it your goal to develop team spirit within your school and especially within your classroom. It's a two-way street. Each student should be made to feel an integral part of the whole, being safe and respected, and each person needs to make the other students feel that same sense of belonging and security.

As Jazz Jennings brought her "Time to Thrive" keynote speech to a close, she said to all the educators in the audience:

> When you have a student who is struggling with gender identity issues, be a mentor. Make them feel safe. Have an open-door policy. Do everything in your power to fight for our right to be treated equally, to be supported, and to be respected for who we are.[44]

Appendix 6

TransKids Purple Rainbow Foundation Goals

TKPRF is committed to the premise that gender dysphoria is something a child can't control, and it is society that needs to change, not them. Families need to support their children and be encouraged to allow them to grow up free of gender roles.

TKPRF is committed to enhancing the future lives of TransKids by educating schools, peers, places of worship, the medical community, government bodies, and society in general, in an effort to seek fair and equal treatment of all trans youth.

TKPRF is committed to funding research to study the current plight and challenges of the trans child. There is an urgent need for curriculum changes in universities and medical schools to meet the needs of all transgender individuals.

TKPRF is committed to supporting TransKids in their school systems so they may receive equal rights in order to ensure a safe and bully-free education.

TKPRF continually uses media outlets to educate and enlighten society, and to challenge injustices due to discrimination.

TKPRF reaches out to the homeless youth and those that have no where else to turn. Funds for healthcare and scholarships can be made available to trans youth in need.

TKPRF is aware that sex and gender are seen and used interchangeably in legal arenas. These two entities are very separate and need to be divided. It is time for the politicians to listen and for the medical professionals to speak up. It is time for the young voices of TransKids everywhere to be heard.

Appendix 7

US Soccer Federation Participation Policy

Following is the USSF policy regarding membership qualifications for recreational soccer leagues, as published on their website: [91]

The United States Soccer Federation (USSF) opens its membership to all soccer organizations and all soccer players, coaches, trainers, managers, administrators and officials "without discrimination on the basis of race, color, religion, age, sex, sexual orientation, gender identity, gender expression or national origin."

For the purposes of registration on gender-based amateur teams, a player may register with the gender team with which the player identifies, and confirmation sufficient for guaranteeing access shall be satisfied by documentation or evidence that shows the stated gender is sincerely held, and part of a person's core identity.

Documentation satisfying the herein stated standard includes, but is not limited to, government-issued documentation or documentation prepared by a healthcare provider, counselor, or other qualified professional not related to the player.

This policy does not apply to Professional Leagues, and does not apply to the Federation's National Teams programs, but application of this or a similar policy shall be re-evaluated at such time as FIFA addresses the issue.

~Jazz Mergirl~

Appendix 8
Guide to Human Sexuality

Following is a more in-depth exploration of human sexuality that may help adult readers better understand this fascinating, but complicated aspect of our lives. There are at least four different elements that combine to make up this complex arrangement.

Birth-Assigned Sex: The first and most obvious element of human sexuality is the *birth-assigned, physical sex* that is recorded on newborns' birth certificates. The designation is primarily based on their genitalia (penis or vagina). Male or female? Until fairly recent times, this is the only aspect of human sexuality that most people in our Western culture consciously thought about. It's what we see, and it's logical to think, "What you see is what you get." Humans like to keep things simple, just two check-boxes, "M" or "F." Turns out that is a mistaken assumption. The reality is *much* more complicated.

Gender Identity: As children get a bit older, they become aware of the second element of human sexuality. That is the internal *gender identity* in their brains. Toddlers as young as one-and-a-half to two-years-old know in their minds whether they relate to being male or female. Observe very young children, and you will see them just naturally gravitate to stereotypical boy or girl toys, behaviors, and even styles of dress. Role models are all around for them to observe and relate to (or reject). It's not something their parents cause to happen. Rather, this is just part of the natural human developmental process.

For most people, this internal, mental gender identity matches their biological, birth-assigned sex, either as male or female. For a very select number of individuals, there is a mismatch between their brains' gender identity and their anatomy. An example is having a girl brain in a boy body, or a boy brain in a girl body. This is called being *transgender*.

For other people, their brains' gender identities are not distinctly male *or* female, but rather a combination of *both* genders (called *gender nonconforming, gender expansive,* or *gender queer*). Others may not identify as *either* gender (called being *agender*). There are even some whose gender identities can vary from day-to-day (*gender fluid*), and people who know their gender identities as male or female, but prefer to appear in both dress and manner as the *opposite* gender (known as *gender variant* or *gender creative*). In fact, there are so many different ways of categorizing gender identities that Facebook profiles now provide almost 60 different gender descriptors for members to choose from. "Ultimately, by changing and broadening our definition of gender identity, we can not only better understand it, we can truly embrace it." [3]

Gender Expression: This brings up a third element of human sexuality called *gender expression* (or *gender presentation)*. That is the way individuals present themselves to the world. It is based on the gender identity in their minds, and includes clothing, hair style, voice, mannerisms, names and pronouns used, choice of playmates and activities, and so forth.

For a number of reasons, many transgender or gender-nonconforming people hide their true gender identity from the world. They instead take on the conventional gender expression that our culture expects for their birth-assigned sex. Males are "supposed" to look and act in certain ways. The same applies for females.

But no matter what façade people put on, or how they act, this in no way alters their deeply-held, internal, gender identity. The result of such secret-keeping and repression is usually a great deal of personal suffering, often leading to life-threatening consequences. Self-harm and suicide rates for such individuals far surpass those of the general population.

Sexual Orientation: The fourth element of sexuality is known as people's *sexual orientation* or *sexual identity*. This is entirely separate from their gender identity (whether gender-normative, trans male, trans female, or gender-nonconforming). Sexual orientation refers to whom people are attracted. Are they straight, gay, bisexual, or pansexual? A person can be transgender and straight, or transgender and gay. A commonly used analogy is that *gender identity* is who you are when you go to bed, while *sexual identity* is who you want in bed with you.

*****

Readers may find the matter of human sexuality to be somewhat confusing. Many people, including some within the LGBTQ community, acknowledge they too are sometimes puzzled about the terminology and concepts associated with this topic. It is recommended that readers go through the Glossary, which follows, for more information that may help answer questions. Additional helpful resources are available online, and many of those are listed in the Resources section toward the back of this book.

*****

What is essential for extending human rights is that people in our culture begin to open up their minds to a more nuanced concept of human sexuality. Trans-advocate Laverne Cox commented about this in a March 2014 *TIME* magazine interview:

> People need to be willing to let go of what they think they know about what it means to be a man and what it means to be a woman. Because that doesn't necessarily mean anything inherently. Folks are just really uncomfortable with that sense of uncertainty, or that shift.[86]

Taking this a step further, trans-model Andreja Pejic stated in her March 2015 *Vogue Magazine* profile that she believes our society is now beginning to accept people in the transgender community, as well as other members of the LGBTQ population.

"There are just more categories now. It's good," said Pejic. "We're finally figuring out that gender and sexuality are more complicated" than we ever thought.[25]

~Jazz Mergirl~

Glossary Notes

The meanings and explanations given in the Glossary that follows are intended to be both accurate and user-friendly, especially for younger readers, rather than being the often less-accessible definitions found in dictionaries or medical texts.

Also, there are a number of extra terms included in the Glossary that are not used in *Jazz Mergirl*. These may be helpful in answering questions that arise from reading the book, and can also serve as a useful reference.

Being *transgender* is a relatively new topic for discussion and study in both the medical and science fields, and within society as a whole. In recent years, this has been the subject of much debate, including within the LGBTQ community itself. As a result, the terminology used is evolving, and it, too, is subject to much discussion and debate.

Glossary

Adolescence: The period in a person's life when they are *mentally* growing from childhood to adulthood. This period of mental change overlaps the time of puberty, when *physical* changes take place. Most define this as age 10–19.

Agender: The individual does not relate to *gender* at all.

Androgynous: Ambiguous appearance or gender expression of a person that includes *both* male and female aspects, such as clothing and hair style.

> Often children appear androgynous. Is that child a boy or girl? An agender, questioning, or gender-nonconforming person may choose an androgynous gender expression.

Birth-Assigned Sex / Biological Sex / Anatomic Sex / Designated Sex: Designating someone as either *male* or *female*, based on their physical characteristics at birth, primarily the genitalia (penis, vagina). This designation or marker is entered on a baby's birth certificate.

Bisexual: A person of one gender who is attracted to both males and females.

Blockers: Prescription drug, usually administered by an endocrinologist, which stops a person's body from producing puberty hormones (testosterone or estrogen).

> Administration of these medications usually begins about age 10–14. This medical intervention prevents puberty-induced physical changes from occurring, while buying time for making longer-term decisions about the transition process.

Blockers may be taken over a much longer time span, even after cross-gender hormone treatment is initiated. (See "cross-gender hormones.")

Cisgender: Refers to a person whose *gender identity* aligns with their *birth-assigned sex*. This term applies to most people.

Coming Out: This means telling others that the person is LGBTQ.

Conventionally Gendered / Gender Normative: An individual's biological sex, gender identity, and gender expression are all in alignment, either being *all* male or *all* female.[61]

Cross-Gender Hormones: Medication that is prescribed by a physician to physically transition a male body into being more female, or transition a female body into being more male.

Diagnosis: A doctor's medical conclusion.

Endocrinologist: Doctor specializing in the body's chemical hormones, including those that make a person have more masculine or more feminine characteristics.

Gay: Over time, this word that originally only referred to males has become a more commonly used, generic term for anyone who identifies as being lesbian, gay, or bisexual. (Homosexual is the older, less preferred term.)

Gay Male: A male who is only attracted to other males.

Gender: A set of qualities and characteristics (expressions) that a culture assigns to each biological sex, male and female. These include expectations for people's appearance, behaviors, activities, and roles in life.

Gender Discord: Synonym for transgender. It means a person's gender identity (*mental*) is different from their birth-assigned sex (*physical*).

Gender Dysphoria: The medical term for a person who is transgender (their gender identity does not match their biological assigned sex / "What's between their ears doesn't match what's between their legs"), *and* the individual experiences an ongoing, significant discomfort (dysphoria) with this situation.

Gender Expression / Gender Presentation: The way people present themselves to the outside world (as opposed to their internal, mental gender identity). These external manifestations include their names, pronouns, clothing, hair style, behavior / mannerisms, voice, and body appearance.

> Society identifies these cues as being masculine, feminine, or androgynous.[20]

> "Many transgender people seek to make their gender expression align with their gender identity, rather than the sex they were assigned at birth." [20]

Gender Fluid / Pangender: Describes an individual whose gender identity changes over time, sometimes even varying from one day to the next, along the *gender spectrum.*

Gender Identity: A person's internal, mental, deeply held sense of their gender.

> For most people, this is either *male* or *female*, and matches their biological sex, but for transgender individuals, their gender identity is different from the sex they were assigned at birth.

> And some other people's gender identity does not fall into the specific categories of male or female, but rather is somewhere in between, called being *gender nonconforming, gender expansive,* or *gender queer*. Or they may be *agender* (not relating to gender

at all). (See "gender spectrum," "gender nonconforming," and "gender fluid.")

Gender Identity Disorder: This is an older medical term for a person whose gender identity does not match their birth-assigned sex (being transgender), *and* who experiences a great deal of discomfort with this condition.

> The term is no longer in use because there was strong opposition to the idea that this is a *disorder*, rather than just how the person happened to be born. See instead the newer term "gender dysphoria." (Jazz Jennings prefers to say she was born "unique" or "special.")

Gender Identity Therapist: Counselor, psychologist, or psychiatrist who specializes in treating patients with issues relating to their gender identity, such as transgender clients.

Gender Nonconforming / Gender Expansive / Gender Variant / Gender Queer:

Describes people whose gender identity is neither *male* nor *female*, but is somewhere in-between, along the *gender spectrum*. Or the person may identify in some other unconventional manner, such as an individual who identifies with their birth-assigned sex, but expresses themself in ways not usually associated with that sex.

> Many in the LGBTQ community say that gender nonconforming is a "third gender," in addition to male and female. Native Americans and other ancient cultures have a concept called "two-spirit," a person whose identity is a blend of male and female.

> Some people are now using the term *gender expansive* rather than *gender nonconforming* because to them, the adjective *nonconforming* has a negative connotation.

The word "queer" was long-considered to be extremely disrespectful and derogatory, but in recent years, some in the younger generation of the LGBTQ community have embraced this adjective in a positive manner. They may even use "queer" as a sort of overall umbrella term for everyone who identifies as being LGBTQIA.

Gender Normative: See "conventionally gendered."

Some argue that the adjective "normative" implies other individuals are "abnormal" instead of just being different from the majority.

Gender Spectrum: In more recent times, this ancient concept has reappeared. It means that human gender is not exclusively "binary" (two) in nature (only male or female), but instead can fall anywhere along a range of gender identities extending all the way from *male* at one end of a continuum, to *female* at the other end of that range.

Genes / Genetic Code: This is nature's code that is built into every cell of every living thing, including humans. Like a computer's programming code, this genetic code instructs and directs how the body develops and functions, including the brain.

Prenatal (before birth) diversity in a baby's gene code causes people to be born with qualities and characteristics that are different from others. These gene-based differences range from physical to mental in nature.

They may be the sort of differences that make each person unique from others in appearance (tall or short, brown or blonde hair, blue or brown eyes, and so forth). Or there may be gene-code irregularities that cause minor inconveniences (such as requiring reading glasses) to major anomalies (such as a being born deaf or having a defective heart valve).

Many medical researchers now believe that rare genetic-code variations may cause some people to have tiny differences in their brain structure that result in their gender identity (*mental*) being misaligned with their birth-assigned sex (*physical*). This is commonly known as "being transgender."

Heterosexual Man or **Woman** / **Straight**: A person whose gender identity matches their birth-assigned sex (male or female), *and* the person's sexual orientation is being attracted to persons of the *opposite* sex. This applies to a majority of the population. (See also "conventionally gendered.")

A trans male attracted to females or a trans female attracted to males is heterosexual.

Homosexual Man or **Woman** / **Gay**: A person whose gender identity matches their birth-assigned sex (male or female), *and* the person's sexual orientation is an attraction to persons of the *same* sex.

A trans male attracted to males or a trans female attracted to females is gay.

Hormones: Chemical messengers that the brain and other organs use to initiate and maintain physical changes (like a boy growing into a man or a girl growing into a woman).

Intersex / **Intergender**: The person's genitals at birth are not clearly one gender or the other, or are both, or do not match the internal reproductive organs.

It is often difficult for the parents and doctors to know how to treat their intersex baby, as a boy, or as a girl. Which way does the child's brain really think? An incorrect assumption can have life-long consequences.

There is a growing trend in the medical community to wait until the person is older and has a clear sense of their gender identity before making any long-term decisions.

LGBTQIA: Acronym for Lesbian – Gay – Bisexual – Transgender – Questioning / Queer – Intersex – Agender. Originally this was the much shorter acronym GLB, but over time, more categories of people have been added.

Lesbian (homosexual is the older, less preferred term): A female who is only attracted to other females. Often the word *gay* is used in place of the term *lesbian*.

MTF / FTM: These acronyms stand for the transition of a Male-to-Female, or of a Female-to-Male.

MTM / FTF: Some transgender people say these two acronyms are preferable because they are not going "from" one birth-assigned gender "to" another, but are instead simply fulfilling the gender they already are in their gender identity. For example, a boy transitioning to a girl (MTF) would instead be considered as a girl becoming the authentic girl she really is inside herself, or FTF.

Pangender: See "gender fluid."

Pansexual: A person whose sexual orientation is to be attracted to others based on their character and personality, rather than being attracted to someone based on their birth-assigned sex, gender identity, or gender expression. This attraction may also be to anyone along the "gender spectrum" who identifies neither distinctly as *male* nor *female*.

Phobia: Intense fear. "Homophobia" means fear and dislike, or even hate, of homosexual individuals, while "transphobia" means fear and loathing of transgender people.

> Such fear and dislike arise about people who are different from the majority of the population. It is said that ignorance breeds fear, and fear breeds hate. Shining a light on such ignorance may open peoples' minds and hearts, making them more

understanding and accepting of those who are different from themselves.

It is unfortunate that some people are so closed-minded that they are simply not able to see anyone else's viewpoint, or even accept the findings of medical science. "My mind is already made up. Don't confuse me with the facts." Jazz Jennings says she always has hope that people can change.

Primary Sex Characteristics: Parts of the body involved in sexual reproduction (making babies), especially the external sex organs commonly referred to as the genitalia or genitals (penis, vagina).

Psychology: The study of how people's minds work, and ways to help them with their mental health. The Greek prefix "psyche" refers to the mind.

Puberty: The stage of human development when the brain begins sending chemical (hormone) messages to the body that initiate changes from that of a child into that of an adult, and over time, male or female characteristics develop.

Queer: See "gender nonconforming."

Secondary Sex Characteristics: Other "non-primary" male or female physical features that appear during puberty, such as changes in bone and muscle structure, body shape, skin texture, and hair growth and texture. (See also "primary sex characteristics.")

Sex: The body's characteristics that indicate a person is physically *male* or *female* primarily based on the genitalia (penis, vagina). (See also "birth-assigned sex.")

Sex Reassignment Surgery (SRS) / **Gender Reassignment Surgery** (GRS), or the newer terms, **Gender Affirmation / Confirmation Surgery**:

These complicated and very costly surgical procedures change the genitals (private parts) of a male to be more like that of a female, or the opposite for a female transitioning to a male. The goal is to bring a person's birth-assigned primary sex characteristics (*physical body*) more into alignment with the individual's gender identity (in the *person's mind*).

> This type of operation has become much more sophisticated since it was first introduced in the 1930's, but the results are still not perfect. This is especially problematic for FTMs.

Sexual Orientation / Sexual Identity: Describes a person's physical, romantic and / or emotional attraction to another person. Is the individual attracted to men, women, both genders, or to those who are gender nonconforming (gender expansive)?

> A transgender person (*gender identity*), just like a nontransgender person, will have a *sexual orientation* (*sexual identity*) that is straight (heterosexual), lesbian, gay, bisexual, pansexual, or asexual.[20]

Stealth / Closeted: Refers to a person with gender identity issues who keeps this a secret from family and / or acquaintances, such as schoolmates or coworkers.

> Or stealth could refer to a person who *has transitioned* and then gets a fresh start in a new location, and chooses to keep their birth-assigned sex confidential. This is called *passing*.

Straight: See "heterosexual."

Transgender: Nonmedical overall "umbrella" term used to describe a person whose gender identity in their mind does not match their body's sex when born (male or female). This gender identity could be the *opposite* of their birth-assigned sex, or the person may identify somewhere along the spectrum between male and female (gender nonconforming / gender expansive), or they could be "agender," meaning the person does not relate to gender at all.

The transgender umbrella includes both those who *have* transitioned in some way or ways (social, chemical, and / or surgical), as well as people who have *not* gone through *any* kind of transition.

An example of such a non-transitioning individual is someone who is "stealth" (living in the shadows), or a child who has not yet begun to transition, or a person who simply chooses not to pursue these procedures.

Note that over time, other groups of people have self-identified as being under the "transgender umbrella," expanding the definition of this descriptor. The result is that its meaning has become less clear, and can be confusing to many others both in and out of the LGBTQ community.

A number of organizations and many transgender people have used *Trans** (*Trans Asterisk*) as shorthand for this umbrella concept.

A common misconception is that being transgender automatically means sex reassignment surgery was performed. That is totally incorrect. (See "transsexual.") Only about one-third of the transgender population elects to have SRS.[86] Others choose not to seek this surgery or simply cannot afford the high cost involved.

Another misunderstanding is the erroneous belief that transgender people are usually gay. In addition to their *gender identity*, a transgender individual, just like everyone else, will also have a *sexual orientation* (*sexual identity*) that may be straight (heterosexual), lesbian, gay, bisexual, pansexual, or asexual.[20]

Transition: The process a transgender person goes through to make changes of a personal / social, medical, and perhaps legal nature so that these aspects of their lives better match the gender they have in their brain (*gender identity*).[20]

> Transitioning is a complex, step-by-step process that occurs over a long period of time.

> Modifications may be made to a person's appearance, physical body, mannerisms, and often their birth name and pronouns (he/she). "Coming out" to family, friends, classmates, and / or coworkers is a common step in transitioning.[20]

> This process is often done with the guidance and assistance of a gender therapist, primary care doctor, and even a surgeon. An attorney may assist with legal matters, such as changing name and gender designation on a birth certificate and other official records, or challenging discriminatory treatment in school or the workplace.

Transsexual: This is an outdated term (now mostly replaced by "transgender") that originated in the medical and psychological communities.

> Some people still prefer this descriptor if they have permanently changed their bodies through medical interventions such as hormones and / or surgery.[20]

Resources

In 2004, when Jeanette Jennings began searching for information and resources online, there was next to nothing on the subject of being transgender, and little in the way of organized support groups. A decade later, the Internet is loaded with websites, blogs, listservs, and organizations ready to help members of the transgender community, their families, and allies.

While the resource listing (below) is fairly extensive, including many of the most prominent sites and organizations, it is still just as a starting point. Any teen or adult with an Internet connection can readily find help and support. It is there for the asking. All information, including Internet links, was current as of publication.

Support and Advocacy Organizations

ACLU LGBT Rights: Working to preserve and protect individual rights in courts, legislatures, and communities. www.aclu.org/lgbt-rights

Best Colleges for LGBT Students: Comprehensive list of colleges that provide an exceptional level of support for students of various gender and sexual identities. www.bestcolleges.com

College Guide for Current and Prospective LGBT Students: Guide to colleges that have adopted a culture of respect for students in the LGBT community. www.accreditedcolleges.com

Center for Transyouth Health and Development (@ Children's Hospital LA)
http://www.chla.org/site/c.ipINKTOAJsG/b.7501767/#.VQD3FuEc39J

Gay-Straight Alliance Network (GSA): Educate schools and communities, advocate for just policies that protect LGBTQ youth from harassment and violence, and organize in coalition with other youth groups across identity lines to address broader issues of oppression. www.gsanetwork.org/

Gender Creative Kids Canada: Providing resources for supporting and affirming gender creative kids within their families, schools and communities. Based in Canada.gendercreativekids.ca

Genderfork: Supportive community for the expression of identities across the gender spectrum. GenderFork.com

Gender Odyssey: Organization dedicated to the education and support of families raising gender variant, gender non-conforming, gender-fluid, cross-gender, and transgender children and adolescents. www.genderodysseyfamily.org/

Gender Spectrum: Provides education, training and support to help create a gender sensitive and inclusive environment for all children and teens. www.genderspectrum.org/

GLAAD (Gay and Lesbian Alliance Against Defamation): Supports the LGBT community by empowering people to share their stories, holding the media accountable for the words and images they present, and helping grassroots organizations communicate effectively.glaad.org/transgender

GLSEN (Gay, Lesbian & Straight Education Network): Leading national education organization focused on ensuring safe schools for all students. http://www.glsen.org

Human Rights Campaign (HRC): Working for lesbian, gay, bisexual, and transgender equal rights. www.hrc.org

It Gets Better: Communicating to lesbian, gay, bisexual, and transgender youth around the world that "It gets better," and to create and inspire the changes that will make it better for members of the LGBTQ community. www.itgetsbetter.org

Kids in the House on Transgender and Gender Non-conforming Youth: Provides an informative series of 1 or 2-minute videos presented by adolescent medicine specialist Dr. Johanna Olson. www.kidsinthehouse.com/expert/parenting-advice-from-johanna-olson-md

Lambda Legal: Oldest and largest national legal organization whose mission is to achieve full recognition of the civil rights of LGBT people through litigation, education, and public policy work. www.lambdalegal.org/issues/transgender-rights

Laura's Playground: Support site for those who are in transition, and for transgender, cross dresser, intersex, and androgynous individuals, their families and friends. www.lauras-playground.com/

Los Angeles Gender Center: Provides an environment of support, understanding, and safety, while helping people explore issues of gender and sexuality. Specializes in gender identity, gender expression, sexual orientation, sexuality, relationships, and intimacy. http://www.lagendercenter.com/about.html

Mermaids (UK): Family support for children and teenagers with gender identity issues. http://www.mermaidsuk.org.uk

Parents of Transgender Children: Facebook group provides a safe place to give and receive support and share in discussions with other parents of trans youth. https://www.facebook.com/groups/108151199217727/

Parents of Transgender Kids: Similar Facebook group. https://www.facebook.com/pages/Parents-of-Transgender-Kids/102798079808117?fref=ts

PFLAG Transgender Network: Support organization specifically for transgender individuals, families and friends. http://community.pflag.org/transgender

Susan's Place: Trans resources. https://www.susans.org/

Teaching Tolerance: Promotes diversity, equal opportunity, and respect for differences in schools. Provides free educational materials to teachers and other school practitioners. www.tolerance.org

Trans Active Gender Center: An internationally recognized non-profit focused on serving the diverse needs of transgender and gender-nonconforming youth, their families, and allies. www.transactiveonline.org/resources/youth/

Trans Family of Cleveland: Family support site. Newsletter, various discussion boards for couples, spouses, parents, and youth. Hundreds of members from all over the world. www.transfamily.org/

TransKids Purple Rainbow Foundation: Committed to enhancing the lives of TransKids by educating schools, peers, places of worship, the medical community, government bodies, and society in general, in an effort to seek fair and equal treatment of all trans youth. www.transkidspurplerainbow.org/ and www.facebook.com/TransKidsPurpleRainbowFoundation

Trans-Parenting.com: Provides support and educational resources to parents and their advocates raising a gender-independent child. Trans-Parenting.com

Trans Youth Equality Foundation: Provides education, advocacy, and support for transgender youth and their families. http://www.transyouthequality.org

Trans Youth Family Allies: Partners with educators, service providers, and communities to develop supportive environments where gender may be expressed and respected. Resources for parents and for youth.
> Parents: www.imatyfa.org/resources/parents/
> Youth: www.imatyfa.org/resources/youth-resources/

Transgender Child: Parent support and resources. transgenderchild.net

Transgender Rainbow Support Group (Santa Ana, CA): An all-inclusive transgender group which provides support to anyone who is transgender or questioning, a friend, or family member, ally, or someone who just wants to understand. www.mach25media.com/tgr.html

The Trevor Project: The leading national organization providing crisis intervention and suicide prevention services to lesbian, gay, bisexual, transgender and questioning (LGBTQ) young people ages 13-24. If you are a youth who is feeling alone, confused, or in crisis, call the Trevor Lifeline at 1-866-488-7386 for immediate help. TheTrevorProject.org

Welcoming Schools (Human Rights Campaign): Offers tools, lessons, and resources for family diversity, avoiding gender stereotyping, and ending bullying and name-calling in elementary schools. http://www.welcomingschools.org

WPATH (World Professional Association for Transgender Health): Devoted to the understanding and treatment of gender identity disorders. www.wpath.org

Blogs

GenderBlog: http://darlenetandogenderblog.com

Gendermom: https://gendermom.wordpress.com/

Raising My Rainbow: raisingmyrainbow.com/

Transparenthood: transparenthood.net/

Books for Young Children

10,000 Dresses. Marcus Ewert. (1 – 3)
A modern fairy tale about becoming the person you feel you are inside. While Bailey dreams of beautiful dresses, no one wants to hear about it because he is a boy. Then an older girl comes along who is inspired by Bailey, and they make beautiful dresses together.

All I Want To Be Is Me. Phyllis Rothblatt. (Pre-K – 3)
Gives voice to the children who don't fit typical gender stereotypes, and who just want to be free to be themselves. Includes children who are fluid in their gender identity and those that feel their body doesn't match who they really are.

Backwards Day. S. Bear Bergman. (2 –3)
An amazing storybook for children, especially good for those whose gender identity differs from their birth-assigned gender. Beautifully illustrated, engaging, and entertaining. Andy's family is relieved after learning there is nothing wrong with their child. He is happier than ever when he can be himself.

Be Who You Are, Jennifer Carr. (1 – 4)
Nick starts school as a boy but draws a self-portrait as a girl because that's how he feels inside. Nick's family shows love and understanding. He works with a gender counselor meeting other children who have similar feelings. Deciding to be called Hope, Hope's parents then work with the school to help with the adjustment.

I am Jazz. Jessica Herthel and Jazz Jennings. (K – 3)
From the time she was two years old, Jazz knew that she had a girl's brain in a boy's body. She loved pink and dressing up as a mermaid and didn't feel like herself in boy's clothing. Based on the real-life experiences of Jazz Jennings.

Jacob's New Dress. Sarah and Ian Hoffman. (Pre-K – 2)
Jacob loves playing dress-up, when he can be anything he wants to be. Some kids at school say he can't wear "girl" clothes, but Jacob wants to wear a dress. Can he convince his parents to let him wear what he wants? Speaks to the unique challenges faced by boys who don't identify with traditional gender roles.

My Princess Boy. Cheryl Kilodavis. (Pre-K – 1)
Dyson loves pink, sparkly things. Sometimes he wears dresses. Sometimes he wears jeans. He likes to wear his princess tiara, even when climbing trees. He's a Princess Boy. Based on a true story.

Oliver Button is a Sissy. Tomie de Paola. (Pre-K – 3)
A little boy must come to terms with being teased and ostracized because he'd rather read books, paint pictures, and tap-dance, instead of participating in sports.

Play Free, McNall Mason and Max Suarez. (Pre-K – 1)
Journey into the life and mind of a young gender-variant boy who wants to be treated fairly and accepted for who he is. Colorful illustrations of assorted beings.

Roland Humphrey is Wearing a WHAT? Eileen Kiernan-Johnson. (K – 3)
The story of a little boy's quest to be his authentic self, dressed in pink and festooned with sparkles, in a world that frowns upon boys who like "girly" things. Based on the author's son's true story.

When Kathy is Keith. Dr. Wallace Wong. (Pre-K – 2)
This story broaches the sensitive and often misunderstood issues that transgender children face. It follows the story of Kathy, a young girl who says she is a boy, but no one takes her seriously.

Resources

When Kayla was Kyle. Amy Fabrikant. (Pre-K – 2)
Kyle doesn't understand why the other kids at school call him names.
He looks like other boys, but doesn't feel like them. Can Kyle find the
words to share his feelings about his gender – and can his parents help
him to transition into the girl he was born to be? Based on real-life
stories.

William's Doll. Charlotte Zolowtow. (Pre-K – 2)
More than anything, William wants a doll. "Don't be a creep," says
his brother. "Sissy, sissy," chants the boy next door. Then one day
someone really understands William's wish, and makes it easy for
others to understand, too.

Books for Teens and Adults

Beyond Magenta – *Transgender Teens Speak Out*. Susan Kuklin.
(Grade 9 +)
A groundbreaking work of LGBT non-fiction takes an honest look at
the life, love, and struggles of transgender teens.

The Boy in the Dress. David Williams. (Grade 5 – 7)
Dennis's dad is depressed since his mom left, and his brother is a
bully. But at least he has soccer. Then he discovers he enjoys wearing
a dress. Told with humor and respect.

Gracefully Grayson. Ami Polonsky. (Grade 5 – 7)
Grayson has been holding onto a secret for what seems like forever.
He is a girl on the inside. Will new strength from an unexpected
friendship and a caring teacher's wisdom be enough to help Grayson?

Luna. Julie Anne Peters. (Grade 9 +)
Liam can't stand the person he is during the day. His female
namesake, his true self, Luna, only reveals herself at night. Now,
everything is about to change. Luna is preparing to emerge from her
cocoon. Compelling and provocative, this is an unforgettable novel
about a transgender teen's struggle for self-identity and acceptance.

Parrotfish. Ellen Wittlinger. (Grade 9+)
Angela has never felt quite right as a girl, but it's a shock to everyone when she cuts her hair short, buys some men's clothes, and announces she'd like to be called by a new name, Grady. Although Grady is happy about his decision, everybody else is having trouble processing the news. In a voice tinged with humor and sadness, Ellen Wittlinger explores Grady's struggles, which any teen will be able to relate to.

None of the Above. I.W. Gregorio. (Grade 9+)
A groundbreaking fiction story about a teenage girl who discovers she's intersex and what happens when her secret is revealed to the entire school. Incredibly compelling, sensitively told, a thought-provoking novel that explores what it means to be a boy, a girl, or something in between.

Rethinking Normal – A Memoir in Transition. Katie Rain Hill. (Grade 9+)
In this first-person narrative, nineteen-year-old Katie Hill shares her personal journey of undergoing gender confirmation surgery. The author reflects on her pain-filled childhood and the events leading up to her life-changing transition.

Riding Freedom. Pam Muñoz Ryan. (Grade 4 – 6)
A fictionalized account of the true story of Charley (Charlotte) Parkhurst, who ran away from an orphanage, lived as a boy, moved to California, and became a stagecoach driver.

Some Assembly Required. Arin Andrews. (Grade 9+)
In his first-person memoir, seventeen-year-old Arin Andrews shares all the hilarious, painful, and poignant details of undergoing gender confirmation surgery. The author details the journey that led him to make this life-transforming decision while still a high school junior.

Books for Parents and Other Adults

Becoming Nicole*:Transformation of an American Family.* Amy Nutt.

The Complicated Geography of Alice. Jules Vilmur.

Gender Born, Gender Made*: Raising Healthy Gender-Nonconforming Children.* Diane Ehrensaft.

Helping Your Transgender Teen. Irwin Krieger.

Middlesex. Jeffrey Eugenides.

Mom, I Need to be a Girl. Just Evelyn. Pdf link: http://ai.eecs.umich.edu/people/conway/TS/Evelyn/Evelyn.html

Raising My Rainbow *– Adventures in Raising a Fabulous, Gender Creative Son.* Lori Duron.

She's Not There*: A Life in Two Genders.* Jennifer Finney Boylan. 2013.

Straight Talk about Sexual Orientation and Gender Identity. Rachel Stuckey.

Trans Forming Families. May Boenke, editor.

Transgender 101. Nicholas Teich.

The Transgender Child*: A Handbook for Families and Professionals.* Stephanie Brill and Rachel Pepper.

Transgender Explained For Those Who Are Not. Joanne Herman.

Transition – The Story of How I Became a Man. Chaz Bono.

Transitions of the Heart *– Stories of Love, Struggle, and Acceptance by the Mothers of Transgender and Gender-Variant Children.* Rachel Pepper, editor.

Adolescent and Teen Camps

Camp Aranu'tiq (New Hampshire and So. California): www.camparanutiq.org/

Camp Born This Way: www.campbornthisway.org/born/

Camp fYrefly: www.fyrefly.ualberta.ca/

Hotlines

Need help or want to talk? These hotlines are always available, 24/7:

The GLBT National Hotline: (888) 843.4564

Trans Lifeline US: (877) 565.8860

Trans Lifeline Canada: (877) 330.6366

The Trevor Project for LGBTQ Youth: (866) 488.7386

~Jazz Mergirl~

Bibliography

Note to the reader: The references below are sequentially numbered. These numbers correspond to the "superscripted" numbers within the text used to designate each citation.

*****

1. Angelo, Mark and Jessica Lynn Cummings. "Jazz and Jeanette – Episode #28." Transition Radio-TV.net. May 12, 2013. YouTube.

2. Anon. "Gay and Transgender Youth Homelessness by the Numbers." Center for American Progress. June 2010.

3. ---. "The Beautiful Way Hawaiian Culture Embraces A Particular Kind Of Transgender Identity." *HuffPost Gay Voices*. Huffington Post.com. April 28, 2015.

4. Arnold, Chris, director. "Trans – the Documentary." RoseWorks and Sex Smart Films. 2012.

4.1 Belzer, Dr. Marvin. Director of the Division of Adolescent and Young Adult Medicine at Children's Hospital Los Angeles. Email conversations with the author. June and July 2015.

5. Brill, Stephanie and Rachel Pepper. *The Transgender Child – A Handbook for Families and Professionals*. 2008.

6. Brittany. "Equality Florida to Honor Jazz Jennings, 14-Year-Old Transgender Advocate." Equality Florida. October 15, 2014.

7. Brittany. "Meet Jazz." Equality Florida. October 23, 2014.

8. Burke, Mary Kathryn. "7 Questions Answered About Transgender People," quoting Dr. Norman Spack. ABC News.go.com. April 24, 2015.

Bibliography

8.1 Carlbert, Michelle. "I Am Jazz's Mom Opens Up." *SheKnows*.com ezine. July 14, 2015.

9. Couric, Katie. "The New Face of Transgender Youth." *Yahoo Global News*. Yahoo News Channel. October 23, 2014. YouTube.

10. Cox, Laverne. "The T Word" documentary. MTV. October 17, 2014.

11. Denton, Elizabeth. "On Struggling To Fit In." *17 Magazine*. March 12, 2015.

11.1 Deutsch, Dr. Maddie. Clinical leader at the UC San Francisco Center of Excellence for Transgender Health. Email conversations with the author. July 2015.

12. Edwards-Stout, Kergan. "The Mother of a Transgender Child Speaks Out." *Gay Voices*. Huffington Post.com. September 11, 2012.

13. English, Bella. "Led by the Child Who Simply Knew." *Boston Globe*. December 11, 2011.

14. Epstein, David. "The Transgender Athlete." *Sports Illustrated*. May 28, 2012.

15. Fabish, Renee. "Video of Transgender Son." February 6, 2015. YouTube.

16. Feeney, Nolan, et. al. "The 25 Most Influential Teens of 2014 – Jazz Jennings, 14." *TIME*. October 13, 2014.

17. Galassi, Josh. "Video: GLAAD Works with Jazz, MTV to Spotlight Trans Youth." GLAAD.org. April 24, 2013. YouTube.

18. Galehouse, Maggie. "Jazz Jennings Shares Story of Her Triumphs and Struggles as a Transgender Child in *I Am Jazz*." *Houston Chronicle Books*. September 12, 2014.

19. George, Allie. "How Teachers Can Support Transgender Students." *The Guardian*. October 29, 2014.

20. GLAAD. "GLAAD Media Reference Guide - Transgender Issues." Glaad.org. n.d.

21. Goldberg, Alan and Joneil Adriano. "I'm a Girl – Understanding Transgender Children." *20/20* transcript. ABC News. April 27, 2007.

22. Goldberg, Leslie. "Jazz Jennings Lands TLC Docuseries." *Hollywood Reporter*. March 12, 2015.

23. Grant, Jaime M., Ph.d, *et al.* "Injustice at Every Turn –The National Transgender Discrimination Survey." National Center for Transgender Equality and National Gay and Lesbian Task Force. 2011.

24. Gray, Eliza. "The Transgender Tipping Point." *TIME*. June 09, 2015.

25. Gregory, Alice. "Has the Fashion Industry Reached a Transgender Turning Point?" *Vogue Magazine*. April 21, 2015.

26. Hartocollis, Anemona. "The New Girl in School: Transgender Surgery at 18." *New York Times*. June 16, 2015.

27. Harvey Milk Foundation & Pride Center Florida. "Diversity Honors." DiversityHonors.com.

28. Hays, Liz. "My Secret Self." *60 Minutes Australia*. April 9, 2009. YouTube.

29. Herthel, Jessica. "Why I Wrote a Book about a Transgender Child." *Huff Post Parents*. Huffington Post.com. September 5, 2014.

30. Herthel, Jessica, and Jazz Jennings. *I Am Jazz*. September 2014.

31. Hill, Katie Rain. *Rethinking Normal*. 2014.

32. Holden, Dominic. "Advice for America from Parents Who support Their Transgender Kids." *Buzzfeed.com*. January 9, 2015.

Bibliography

33. Human Rights Campaign (HRC). "Time to Thrive – About the Conference." TimeToThrive.org. February 2015.

34. ---. "Transgender Children & Youth: Understanding the Basics." HRC.org. n.d.

35. Jennings, Greg and Jeanette Jennings. "How Barbara Walters Saved Our Family." Op-Ed. *Advocate.com* September 24, 2014.

36. Jennings, Jazz. "7-Year-Old Jazz – Thoughts on Being Transgender." GnetLuvsGreg on YouTube. June 27, 2008.

36.1 ---. "11-Year-Old Transgender Girl Jazz, Message to Obama." GnetLuvsGreg on YouTube. May 24, 2012.

37. ---. "About Us" and "FAQ." Jazzmergirl.wix.com/ PurpleRainbowTails.

38. ---. "Clean and Clear – See the Real Me" ad campaign. Johnson & Johnson Co. March, 2015. YouTube.

39. ---. Colin Higgins Youth Courage Award acceptance speech. Trevor Project. Jazz Jennings on YouTube. June 25, 2012.

40. ---. "DIY: Silicone Mermaid Tail Scales / Part 1." Jazz Jennings on YouTube. April 2, 2014.

40.1---. *I Am Jazz* docuseries. TLC TV. July 2015.

41. ---. "Jazz a Transgender Child: Letter to the World." Jazz Jennings on YouTube. July 16, 2014.

42. ---. "Jazz a Transgender Child: Q & A." Jazz Jennings on YouTube. July 27, 2014.

43. ---. "Jazz a Transgender Child: Q & A" posted comments. Jazz Jennings on YouTube. September 2014.

44. ---. "Jazz Jennings at the 2015 HRC Foundation's Time to Thrive Conference – Youth Advocate Keynote Speech." HRC on YouTube. February 13, 2015.

45. ---. LGBT Pride Month remarks at The White House. facebook.com / White House/videos. June 24, 2015.

45.1---. Panel discussion. Outfest Film Festival Appearance. July 12, 2015.

46. ---. Posting on "Jazz Jennings – Public Figure" page. Facebook.com.

47. ---. Posting on "Jazz Jennings" Twitter page. Twitter.com. June 10 – 11, 2015.

48. ---. Purple Rainbow Tails (Small Business Page). Facebook.com.

48.1---.Purple Rainbow Tails "FAQ." PurpleRainbowTails.com.

49. ---. "Purple Rainbow Tails – Changing the World One Tail at a Time." Indiegogo.com.

50. ---. Q & A. ask.fm. 2014-2015.

51. ---. "Transgender Teen Speaks at Equality Florida." Equality Florida Award acceptance speech. Jazz Jennings on YouTube. November 16, 2014.

52. ---. Twitter live chat. *Out There*. MSNBC's Shift network. March 25, 2015.

53. Jennings, Jeanette. TransKids Purple Rainbow Foundation (TKPRF) website.

54. Jennings, Jeanette and Deborah Grayson. "Episode #10 – TransKids Purple Rainbow Foundation Interview." *Transwaves Podcast*. Trans Youth Equality Foundation. 2014.

Bibliography

55. Kendall, Jonathan Kendall. "Jazz Jennings Honored by Equality Florida." *Broward-Palm Beach New Times*. October 31, 2014.

56. Khan, Yasmeen. "A Child Moves from He to She with Confidence." WNYC.org. June 8, 2015.

57. Koman, Tess. "Leelah Alcorn Suicide." *Cosmopolitan.com*. December 30, 2014.

58. Liao, Marina. "This 14-Year-Old Transgender Girl Will Change Your View of Beauty." *Popsugar.com*. March 12, 2015.

59. Logo TV. "Youth Trailblazer Award – Jazz Jennings" video. Logotv.com. 2014.

59.1 Lowry, Brian. "TV Review: I Am Jazz." *Variety*. July 13, 2015.

60. Mack, Marlo. Op-ed: "Finally, Some Reliable Research on Trans Kids Like Mine." *Advocate.com*. February 11, 2015.

60.1 ---. "Podcast VII – The Facts (about Transgender Kids)." *How to be a Girl Podcast.com*. June 30, 2015.

61. Mazzella, Randi. "How to Support Your Transgender Teen." *TeenLife Blog.com* December 18, 2014.

62. McNicholas, Shelagh. "About Me." ShelaghMcNicholas.co.uk. 2015.

63. Mendez, Alicia. "12-Year-Old Jazz Discusses Life Growing Up Trans." *Huff Post Live*. Huffington Post.com. April 2, 2013.

64. Menendez, Alicia, and Ignacio Torres. "Meet Jazz: The 14-Year-Old Face of the Trans Community." *AM Tonight*. Fusion TV. October 30, 2014.

64.1 Menendez, Alicia, with Meagan Redman and Lauren Effron. "I Am Jazz: Transgender Teen on Grappling with High School, Puberty." *Nightline*. ABC News.com. July 14, 2015.

65. Mock, Janet. "I Am Jazz – My Intimate Conversation with Trans Tween Jazz & Her Mother Jeanette." *Janet Mock.com*. November 25, 2011.

66. Newman, Andrew Adam. "Clean & Clear Videos." *New York Times*. March 12, 2014.

67. Nichols, James Michael. "Jazz Jennings, Transgender Teen, Becomes Face of Clean & Clear Campaign." *Huff Post Style*. Huffington Post.com. March 14, 2015.

68. Nyberg, Renée. Interview with Jazz Jennings and family. Swedish TV3. March 2014. YouTube.

69. O'Donnell, Rosie. Interview with Jazz and Jeanette Jennings. *The Rosie Show*. Oprah Winfrey Network (OWN). November 14, 2011.

70. Olson, Dr. Johanna. "My Videos." Kids in the House.com. 2015.

71. Parrott, Kiera. "A New Picture Book Biography about a Transgender Girl." *School Library Journal*. August 25, 2014.

72. Pepper, Rachel, editor. *Transitions of the Heart*. 2012.

73. Pinsky, Dr. Drew. "A Child in Transition." *Dr. Drew Show*. HLN TV. November 23, 2011. YouTube.

74. Pompei, Vincent. "Human Rights Campaign Youth Ambassadors – Jazz Jennings." HRC.org. 2014.

74.1 Poniewozik, James. "An Extraordinary, Ordinary Girlhood in TLC's *I Am Jazz*." *TIME*.com. July 15, 2015.

75. Price, Michael. Interview with the author. January 7, 2015.

76. Redd, Nancy. "Transgender Teen Jazz Jennings Live." *Huff Post Live*. Huffington Post.com. March 23, 2015.

77. Rice, Lynette. "Meet the Transgender Teen from I Am Jazz." *Entertainment Weekly*. June 1, 2015.

Bibliography

77.1 Roberts, Thomas. "One-on-One with Jazz Jennings, Teenage Transgender Advocate." *Out There*. Shift Network Online. MSNBC.com. March 25, 2015.

78. Rodriguez, Laura. "Transgender Teen Writes Kid's Book to Help Others." NBC 6 TV Miami.com. June 25, 2014.

79. Rothaus, Steve. "Equality Florida Voice of Equality Award." *Miami Herald*. October 15, 2014.

80. ---. "Growing up Transgender: Jazz Jennings." *Miami Herald – Palette Magazine*. June 25, 2015.

81. Ruiz, Michelle. "Jazz Jennings: The Transgender Teen and Wannabe Mermaid the Internet Needs." *Cosmopolitan.com*. June 8, 2015.

82. Sargent, Irika. "South Florida Teenager Tackles Difficult Issue of Transgender." CBS-Miami. September 21, 2014.

83. Seaman, Andrew M., "Transgender Youth Identity Reveals Significance of Parental Acceptance." *Huffington Post Gay Voices*. February 20, 2015.

84. Smith, Dianna. "All That Jazz." *Boca Raton Observer*. August 2014.

85. Stafford, Claire. "Equality Ally Award." Equality California. Vimeo. June 1, 2013.

86. Steinmetz, Katy. "Laverne Cox Talks to *TIME* About the Transgender Movement." *TIME*. May 29, 2014.

87. Stocks, Jennifer – Director. *I Am Jazz: A Family in Transition*. OWN TV. November 27, 2011. YouTube.

87.1 Tando, Darlene. LCSW, Gender Therapist. Email conversations with the author. July 2015.

88. Teich, Nicholas. *Transgender 101 – A Simple Guide to a Complex Issue*. 2012, and "Transgender 101: 15 Things to Know." *Huffington Post Gay Voices*. Huffington Post.com. April 18, 2012.

89. Thompson, Linda. "How Living With and Loving Bruce Jenner Changed My Life Forever," *Huffington Post Gay Voices*. April 29, 2015.

90. Trimarchi, Maria. "How Gender Identity Disorder Works." How Stuff Works.com. n.d.

91. United States Soccer Federation. "Participation Policy." USSoccer.com.

92. Vieira, Meredith. *Meredith Vieira Show*. NBC TV. March 25, 2015. YouTube.

92.1 Villarreal, Yezmin. "I Am Jazz: 14, Transgender, and the Star of My Own Docuseries." July 29, 2015. *The Advocate*.

93. Walsh, Jim. "Transgender High School Athlete – All Kids Deserve to be Happy." *Minnesota Post.com*. December 4, 2014.

94. Walters, Barbara. "My Secret Self." *20/20*. ABC TV. April 27, 2007. YouTube.

95. ---. "Transgender at 11: Listening to Jazz." *20/20*. ABC TV. June 19, 2013. YouTube.

96. Wikipedia. "Gender Identity Disorder." *Wikipedia.com*. 2015.

97. Williams, Cristan. "*I Am Jazz*: An Amazing Book for Trans Kids." *TransAdvocate.com*. September 14, 2014.

98. Wilson, Cintra. "The Reluctant Transgender Role Model." *New York Times.com*. May 6, 2011.

99. Woog, Dan. "US Soccer and All That Trans Jazz." *Between the Lines News*. March 7, 2013.

100. Zack, S. "When Is Young Too Young?" *The Reporter*. March 2006.

101. Zuckerman, Alicia. "New Children's Book Looks at What It's Like to be a Transgender Kid." WLRN FM – Miami. Oct. 9, 2014.

Acknowledgments

The process of writing and publishing *Jazz Mergirl* has been a long, challenging, exciting, and most-fulfilling journey. A number of people helped me along my way, and now that this project has come to fruition, I want to recognize their assistance.

After writing a substantial portion of the book, one of the first people with whom I shared this was Gary B. North, a journalist and copy editor. A dedicated supporter of the LGBT community, Gary was quick to offer his time and expertise in reviewing my initial rough draft. He provided valuable, detailed feedback on issues of style and grammar, the result of which is a more polished and professional final version. We had some rather lively debates, and his influence is especially present in my numerous "Notes to the Reader." If I were to "break some rules," I needed to make sure readers knew why. GBN, thanks for all your help.

Dr. Jaelline Jaffe is another individual who played an important role in my *Jazz Mergirl* project. She has been a strong and enthusiastic supporter of this venture ever since I first shared it with her, giving most generously of her time and advice. Like Gary, Dr. Jaffe was a significant influence on matters of style and grammar. She provided very helpful feedback on the portions of the book that she reviewed, including pointing out awkward phrasing or grammatical structure in need of revision. In addition, Dr. Jaffe gave suggestions that greatly improved the visual appearance of this book. A prominent Marriage and Family Therapist, author, and former educator, Dr. Jaffe's background and experience enabled her to provide me with invaluable guidance and thought-provoking ideas as well. I thank you so very much, Dr. J.

One more grammarian deserves recognition. Tessie Edlen, the "thoughtful 95-year-old lady" quoted in Chapter 23, is sometimes referred to as "Typo Tessie" for her decades-long crusade to get local newspapers to do a better job editing their copy. A longtime ally of people she knows in the LGBT community, she was excited and enthusiastic to read portions of *Jazz Mergirl*, and gave useful observations and numerous suggestions (as well as correcting errors in grammar). Thanks Mom.

I also sought comments and feedback about the front matter of the manuscript. Dr. Alison Townsend, Ph.d, is a long-time friend and Emerita Professor of English at the University of Wisconsin. She responded with some very useful proposals that helped me improve the Preface and Introduction. In addition, Dr. Townsend was most encouraging about the project as a whole, and about the quality of the writing in particular. For a first-time author, hearing that response was quite affirming and validating. Alison, I am so pleased to call you my friend after so many years.

In addition, I reached out to another maven of fine writing, the distinguished children's book consultant and lecturer Janet Zarem. She graciously offered her time and guidance in support of this project that she so enthusiastically embraced. We spent quite some time emailing and on the phone discussing various aspects of the manuscript, and Janet's expertise in both the realm of the publishing world and good writing proved most beneficial. I felt much more knowledgeable and confident as a result. Janet, I am so appreciative of your assistance.

I owe a debt of gratitude to Lori Duron, mother of CJ, and author of the wonderful blog and book, *Raising My Rainbow*. She has been very kind in responding to both my questions and concerns as a first-time author. Lori's work inspired portions of the back matter in *Jazz Mergirl*, as noted in the text, and elements of her website gave me ideas on how to set that up for this book. Thank you so much, Lori Duron.

A huge thank you goes to Dr. Marvin Belzer, MD, for taking time out from his demanding practice to review the medical aspects of the *Jazz Mergirl* manuscript. I wanted to ensure that this book accurately and clearly presents this most essential aspect of Jazz's story. Dr. Belzer is an internationally recognized leader in the field of transgender care for youth, and Director of the Division of Adolescent and Young Adult Medicine at Children's Hospital Los Angeles, and is associated with the Center for Transyouth Health and Development at CHLA, directed by Dr. Johanna Olson, MD. Many thanks to you, Dr. Belzer, and to Dr. Jo for her dedication to the trans youth community, and for the transgender research studies she is conducting. In this same regard, I am most appreciative for the time and helpful input provided to me by Darlene Tando, LCSW. Thank you for validating and supporting this project.

Acknowledgments

I want to recognize several others who responded to my requests for input about some of the book's front matter and the book cover. They all came through with helpful comments and suggestions, along with their encouragement and support for this project: Wendy, Daniel and Brit, Jordana, Bev and Oliver, Michelle, and Susan. Lorna Collins, author, was most kind in giving me both encouragement, and excellent advice for improving the back cover. And I appreciate the information provided by my friend Marcia, who already has a book in print. Thanks to each one of you for your help along the way to publishing *Jazz Mergirl.*

And finally, I want to express my deep gratitude to my graphic designers, J&J, whose skills, creativity, and patience led to the iconic, eye-catching *Jazz Mergirl* front cover, the final version of the back cover, and the design and implementation of the book's website. These crucial elements will go a long way to making *Jazz Mergirl* a success, and allow me to be of greater support to the TransKids Purple Rainbow Foundation. JR, I'll never forget your comment to me that got you involved: "You know, you don't have to do this all by yourself!" I am most grateful for your vital assistance.

Long ago, I promised myself that if I ever published something, it would include special recognition for two exceptional people in my life. To Anne, my fifth-grade teacher and her then fiancé, Dr. Stephen T., who provided a safe haven for a troubled little boy in great need. Thank you, with much love and gratitude. I have tried to "pay it forward" with my own students.

~Jazz Mergirl~

To Mike McCance, my dear friend and mentor, whose lessons in the art of education and in life so inspired me and informed my own teaching. She lives on in my life, and in the lives of so many of my students, and all the children she taught over the years. And Jacque Nunez, I am grateful for the example of respect and dignity you gave to me and my students. For many subsequent years, I continued to pass along that same lesson.

Finally, this is for you, Jazz Mergirl. I love you dearly. I'm so proud of you, and I wish you and your family the best always.

Bruce Edlen
August 2015

Made in the USA
San Bernardino, CA
07 December 2015